Mark Ravenhill

pool (no water)
and
Citizenship

Methuen Drama

Published by Methuen Drama 2006

3 5 7 9 10 8 6 4 2

Methuen Drama
A & C Black Publishers Limited
38 Soho Square
London W1D 3HB
www.acblack.com
Copyright © 2006 by Mark Ravenhill

Mark Ravenhill has asserted his right under the Copyright, Designs
and Patents Act, 1988, to be identified as the author of this work

A CIP catalogue record for this book is available from the British Library

ISBN: 978 0 7136 8398 1

Typeset by Country Setting, Kingsdown, Kent
Printed and bound in Great Britain by
MPG Books Ltd, Bodmin, Cornwall

Caution

All rights whatsoever in these plays are strictly reserved.
Application for all performance rights in the United Kingdom
including amateur performances should be addressed to
Casarotto Ramsay and Associates Limited, Waverley House,
7–12 Noel Street, London W1F 8GQ (agents@casarotto.uk.com)

No performance shall be given unless a licence has been obtained.

All rights reserved. No part of this publication may be reproduced
in any form or by any means – graphic, electronic or mechanical, including
photocopying, recording, taping or information storage and retrieval systems –
without the written permission of A & C Black Publishers Limited.

This book is produced using paper that is made from wood grown
in managed, sustainable forests. It is natural, renewable and recyclable.
The logging and manufacturing processes conform to the environmental
regulations of the country of origin.

A Frantic Assembly, Drum Theatre Plymouth and Lyric Hammersmith Production

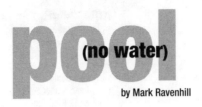

(no water)

by Mark Ravenhill

The first performance of **pool (no water)** took place on Friday 22nd
September 2006 at the Drum Theatre Plymouth.

UK Tour Autumn 2006

Drum Theatre Plymouth	22 September – 07 October
Everyman Theatre, Liverpool	10 October – 14 October
Contact Theatre, Manchester	17 October – 21 October
Lyric Hammersmith, London	31 October – 18 November
The Point, Eastleigh	21 November – 23 November

A free resource pack for **pool (no water)** is available to download from
www.franticassembly.co.uk. The website also contains information on a special
programme of workshops and teachers INSET's to accompany **pool (no water)**
and details of forthcoming training sessions open to all.

Frantic Assembly
31 Eyre Street Hill
London EC1R 5EW
020 7841 3115
admin@franticassembly.co.uk

Registered Charity No. **1113716**
Registered Company No. **2989694**

A Frantic Assembly, Drum Theatre Plymouth and Lyric Hammersmith Production

pool
(no water)
by Mark Ravenhill

Cast	Keir Charles
	Cait Davis
	Leah Muller
	Mark Rice-Oxley

Creative Team

Writer	**Mark Ravenhill**
Direction and choreography	**Scott Graham and Steven Hoggett**
Design	**Miriam Buether**
Lighting Design	**Natasha Chivers**
Music	**Imogen Heap**
Film	**Jacob Love**
Casting Director	**Julia Horan**

Production Team

Production Manager	**John Titcombe**
Company Stage Manager	**Joni Carter**
Technical Stage Manager	**Andy Purves**
Assistant Stage Manager	**Emma Barrow**
Production Runner	**Fiona Clift**

For Drum Theatre Plymouth

Production Manager	**David Miller**
Costume Supervisor	**Lydia Hardiman**
Sets, Props and Costumes	**TR2 - Theatre Royal Plymouth Production Centre**

For Frantic Assembly

Producer	**Lisa Maguire**
Administrator	**Laura Sutton**
Marketing	**Jill Cotton - Chamberlain AMPR**
Press	**Ben Chamberlain - Chamberlain AMPR**
Photography	**Sam Barker**
Graphic Design	**feastcreative.com**
	polymathdesign.co.uk

Developed at BAC and the National Theatre Studio

Frantic Assembly would like to thank:

Amanda Lawrence, Ian Goldin, Tam Ward, Daniel Evans, Abby Ford, Hayley Carmichael & Burn Gorman. Simon Stokes, Paul Clay, Jessica Hepburn and David Farr. The Tab Centre. Leon Baugh (for the best bounce), Rufus Norris (for being true to his word) and Mary Teasdale (mam-gu extraordinaire). Gordon Millar and Sinead Mac Manus.

Biographies

Scott Graham Artistic Director

Scott is Artistic Director and co-founder of Frantic Assembly. Director/performer credits for the company include Hymns, On Blindness, Tiny Dynamite, Heavenly, Sell Out, Zero, Flesh, Klub, and Look Back in Anger. For Frantic Assembly Scott has co directed Dirty Wonderland, Rabbit, Peepshow and Underworld. Scott's other directing credits include Home (National Theatre of Scotland) and It's A Long Road (Polka Theatre). Choreography and movement director credits include; Market Boy (National Theatre), Villette (Stephen Joseph Theatre), Vs (Karim Tonsi Dance Company Cairo), Improper (Bare Bones Dance Company), Dazzling Medusa and A Bear Called Paddington (Polka Theatre) and Stuart Little (Ambassadors Theatre Group).

Steven Hoggett Artistic Director

Steven is Artistic Director and co-founder of Frantic Assembly. As director and/or performer he has been involved in every Frantic production, most recently Hymns and Dirty Wonderland (Brighton Festival). Additional performance credits include Volcano Theatre Company and The Featherstonehaughs. Steven's choreography and movement director credits include Black Watch and Wolves In The Walls (National Theatre of Scotland), Market Boy (National Theatre), Villette (Stephen Joseph Theatre), Jerusalem (West Yorkshire Playhouse), Mercury Fur and The Straights (Paines Plough) and the award-winning Orange television commercial Relationships Dance.

Mark Ravenhill Writer

Mark Ravenhill's first full-length play Shopping and Fucking was produced by Out Of Joint and the Royal Court Theatre and opened at the Ambassadors in 1996. Faust is Dead was produced by the Actors Touring Company in 1997. Handbag was produced by ATC in 1998 and his next play, Some Explicit Polaroids for Out Of Joint, opened at the New Ambassadors Theatre in 1999. Mother Clap's Molly House opened at the National Theatre in 2001 and transferred to the West End in 2002. Mark wrote and performed his one-man show Product at the Edinburgh Fringe Festival, then at the Royal Court Theatre London in 2005 and is currently on tour throughout Europe. The Cut opened at the Donmar Warehouse in February 2006, starring Sir. Ian McKellen and directed by Michael Grandage. Citizenship, a play for teenagers, opened at the National Theatre in March 2006.

Miriam Buether Designer

Miriam trained in costume design at Akademie für Kostüm Design in Hamburg and in theatre design at Central Saint Martins. She was the overall winner of the 1999 Linbury Prize and won the 2004/5 Critics Award for Theatre in Scotland for The Wonderful World of Dissocia. Design credits for theatre and dance include Realism (National Theatre of Scotland and Edinburgh International Festival 2006), Unprotected (Liverpool Everyman and Traverse Edinburgh), Trade (RSC New Work Festival and Soho Theatre), The Bee (Soho Theatre and Noda Map Tokyo) The Death of Kinghoffer (Edinburgh International Festival 2005 and Scottish Opera), After the End (Traverse Theatre and tour Germany/Balkans), Way to Heaven (Royal Court), Platform (ICA), The Wonderful World of Dissocia (Edinburgh International Festival 2004, Drum Plymouth, Tron Glasgow), Tender Hooks, and Outsight (Foundation Gulbenkian, Lisbon), Guantanamo (Tricycle Theatre, West End London and NY), Track (Scottish Dance Theatre), The Dumb Waiter and Other Pieces (Oxford Playhouse), Body Of Poetry (Komische Oper Berlin), People Next Door (Traverse Edinburgh and NY), Red Demon (Young Vic and Noda Map Tokyo), Bintou (Arcola Theatre), Possibly Six, and TOOT (Grand Ballets de Canadiens) 7DS (Sadler's Wells).

Natasha Chivers Lighting Designer

Recent work includes: Mary Stuart (National Theatre of Scotland), Sunday In The Park With George (Wyndhams Theatre), Encore (George Piper Dances at Sadlers Wells), Wolves In The Walls (Improbable/National Theatre Of Scotland/Lyric Hammersmith/Tour), HOME (National Theatre Scotland), A Fine Balance (Tamasha -Hampstead Theatre), Jerusalem and My Mother Said I Never Should (West Yorkshire Playhouse), Renaissance (Greenwich and Docklands International Festival), Dirty Wonderland (Frantic Assembly/Brighton Festival), Who's Afraid Of Virginia Woolfe (Liverpool Playhouse),Hymns (Frantic Assembly/Lyric Hammersmith/tour), The Paines Plough Season at The Chocolate Factory including Mercury Fur (with Plymouth Drum), Small Things, Pyrenees (with The Tron Theatre Glasgow), If Destroyed Still True (with Dundee Rep); Beauty Queen Of Leenane (Watford Palace Theatre), Liverpool Everyman 40th Anniversary Season including Urban Legend and The Kindness Of Strangers. Unexpected Man (Bath Theatre Royal Productions/Tour). Other work includes: The Bomb-itty of Errors (The New Ambassadors),The Straits (59 East 59, New York, Hampstead Theatre), Ma Rainey's Black Bottom and The Entertainer (Liverpool Playhouse); Who's Afraid Of The Big Bad Book (Soho Theatre/Warwick Arts Centre); The Cherry Orchard and After The Dance (Oxford Stage Company -tour); Present Laughter (Bath Theatre Royal Productions), Playhouse Creatures (West Yorkshire Playhouse); Peepshow (Frantic Assembly, Plymouth Theatre Royal, Lyric Hammersmith and tour), The Drowned World (Paines Plough, Traverse Theatre and Bush Theatre); Tiny Dynamite (Frantic Assembly, Paines Plough, Lyric Hammersmith and International tour).

Imogen Heap Music

2006 has proved a remarkable year for IMOGEN HEAP. Her latest album 'Speak For Yourself' is close to 200,000 sales in the US, and with performances on every major US chat show during her last sold-out US tour in May (including Letterman, Carson and Leno), the Brit singer/songwriter/producer is looking like being one of the UK's biggest exports to the United States this year.   In the UK, she has sold out two full tours, with a third tour – her biggest yet with a mammoth 14 dates - scheduled across October and November.   She scored her very first Record Of The Week on Radio 1, built a Myspace following which puts Madonna and the Arctic Monkeys to shame and recorded the theme to the biggest Christmas cinema blockbuster (The Chronicles Of Narnia). On 2nd October 2006, White Rabbit Recordings through Sony BMG release the brand new single 'Headlock', one of the stand out tracks from her latest album, 'Speak For Yourself'. Imogen recently recorded a very special a cappella version of the Leonard Cohen classic 'Hallelujah' which, for the second year running, secured Imogen the prime music slot over the climatic scene to the season three finale of the hit teen drama The OC, again attracting a brand new audience of teenage music fans. Unavailable for download when the episode aired, another original Imogen composition 'Speeding Cars', used in the same episode, attracted a huge 40,000 download sales shortly after broadcast. After this, she travelled to Africa to begin work on her first film score, due for release in 2007. After recently meeting him backstage at one of her LA gigs, Zach Braff has used the lead track 'Hide And Seek' from Imogen's latest album 'Speak For Yourself' on the soundtrack to his latest film 'The Last Kiss', co-starring The OC's Rachel Bilson, and out in UK cinemas from Oct 26th. Coincidentally, the same song provided Imogen with her worldwide commercial breakthrough when used on The OC in the key music slot in their Season Two finale.

Jacob Love Visual Artist

Jacob Love is an artist who works in still and moving imagery, using digital video, photography, found images, objects and writing. His practice dwells on the inadequacy of photographic and video image to represent the power of human experience. Looking at instances where images fail in their representations, his work sets out to blur the distinction between recorded, remembered and imagined imagery. His work challenges our perceived notions of how images function in the creation and maintenance of memory. The repeated use of personal imagery from Jacobs own past acknowledges the sentimentality and vanity involved in recording and displaying our lives visually, and our tendency to mould experiences into clichéd images in order to give them meaning.   Jacob has been involved in numerous exhibitions, and publications and lives in London.

Julia Horan CDG Casting Director

Recent credits include: All About My Mother (Neal St/Old Vic), Gaddaffi (ENO/Asian Dub Foundation), Rabbit (Old Red Lion/Trafalgar Studios), Tintin (Young Vic/Barbican), A Brief History of Helen of Troy (ATC), The Prayer Room (Birmingham Rep/EIF), As You Like It (Wyndhams); One Under (Tricycle); Anna in the Tropics, Yellowman (Hampstead); Othello (Cheek by Jowl), The Skin of our Teeth, Hobson's Choice, The Daughter-in-law, Homebody Kabul, A Raisin in the Sun, Six Characters Looking for an Author, (Young Vic); The Morris, Port Auhtority, Urban Legend, The Kindness of Strangers (Liverpool Everyman); The Girl on the Sofa (EIF/Schaubuhne Theatre, Berlin); Original Sin (Crucible, Sheffield); Antartica (Savoy); The Weir (Duke of York's); The Force of Change, Made of Stone, Local, Trade, About a Boy, Yardgal, Holy Mothers, Last Dance at Dum-Dum (Royal Court).

Keir Charles Performer

Keir trained at Central School of Speech and Drama. Theatre credits include: On the Piste (Birmingham Rep), Incomplete and Random Acts of Kindness (Royal Court), Baal (workshop – Young Vic), Romeo and Juliet (Liverpool Everyman), Eye Contact (Riverside Studios), Keepers (Hampstead), and Cadillac Ranch (Soho Theatre). Television work includes Oliver in both series of The Green Wing (Talkback Productions), Fear of Fanny (BBC), HG Wells – A Life in Picture (Wall to Wall), Our Hidden Lives (Diverse Productions), The Bill (Thames Television), Dirty War (BBC), Family Business (Tiger Aspect), Holby City and Ed Stone is Dead (BBC). Film credits include High Heels, Low Life (Fragile Films) and Love Actually (Working Title). Short films: Sand, What Larry Says, Indecision. Radio: Intent to Supply.

Cait Davis Performer

Theatre credits include: Wolves In The Wall (National Theatre Of Scotland/Lyric Hammersmith/ Tour), The Little Fir Tree (Crucible Studio Theatre), Measure For Measure (Complicite, RNT), Top Girls (Citizens Theatre, Glasgow),Those Eyes, That Mouth, and Fermentation (Gridiron Theatre Company), The Chimp That Spoke, Mosquito Coast (David Glass Ensemble), How To Behave (Station House Opera/Hampstead Theatre), Running Girl, Red (Boilerhouse); 1984 (Northern Stage Ensemble), Phantom Limb (Theatre Gargantua), Into Our Dreams (Almeida Theatre), Scratch (20:21 Productions), The Carrier Frequency (Stans Cafe). For Frantic Assembly Cait has performed in Klub, Flesh, Sell Out, Zero and Dirty Wonderland. Cait made her television debut playing the role of Brown in Respectable Trade for the BBC.

Leah Muller Performer

Leah trained at the Guildhall School of Music and Drama. Theatre includes: Romans in Britain (Sheffield Crucible), The Tempest (Liverpool Playhouse), The Crucible (Birmingham Rep), Paradise Lost (Theatre Royal Northampton), The Girl on the Sofa (Edinburgh International Festival/Schaubuhne Theatre Berlin), Six Characters Looking for an Author (Young Vic – Olivier nomination), The Seagull (Theatre Royal Northampton), Hayfever (Oxford Stage Company), The House of Bernarda Alba (Orange Tree), Frankenstein (National Theatre Studio), The Old Curiosity Shop (Drill Hall workshop), Arms and the Man and The Captain's Tiger (Orange Tree Theatre). Opera: The Trojans (ENO). Film: Vagabond Shoes (Jackie Udney), A Touch of Sadness (Nicola Mills). TV includes: The Bill, Casualty and Man and Boy.

Mark Rice-Oxley Performer

Mark trained at Webber Douglas. Theatre credits include: Romans in Britain (Sheffield Crucible), The Life of Galileo (Birmingham Rep), David Copperfield (West Yorkshire Playhouse), The Kindness of Strangers (Liverpool Everyman), The Entertainer (Liverpool Playhouse), The Comedy of Errors (Bristol Old Vic),Cuckoos (Barbican Pit and Ustinov Studio Bath), The Dwarfs (Tricycle Theatre), Workers Writes (Royal Court), The Danny Crowe Show (Bush Theatre), Cressida (Albery Theatre). Film/TV includes: George Harrison in The John Lennon Story (NBC), The Dwarfs, Mersey Beat, Judge John Deed, Two Pints of Lager and a Packet of Crisps and In Deep (all BBC). Radio includes: Four For A Boy, The Rakes's Progress, Kaleido (all BBC).

John Titcombe Production Manager

From 1996 to 2005 John was Production Manager at Hampstead Theatre. Since then projects have included Look Back In Anger (Theatre Royal Bath), My Fair Lady (Larnaca International Festival, Cyprus), Present Laughter (UK Tour), Pericles and Invisible Mountains (National Theatre education tour), Mammals (Bush Theatre & UK Tour), Longitude (Greenwich Theatre), Playing with Fire (Olivier Theatre), Aristocrats (Lyttelton Theatre), What the Butler Saw (Criterion Theatre), Losing Louis (Trafalgar Studios) and Bat Boy the Musical (Shaftesbury Theatre). Future projects include Woyzeck (St Ann's Warehouse New York).

Joni Carter Company Stage Manager

Joni works as a freelance stage manager on theatre projects and live events, with a keen interest in devised and site specific projects. She was company stage manager with Theatre O, touring internationally to festivals with Three Dark Tales and The Argument. Joni has collaborated with the Unicorn Theatre, Theatre-Rites, National Theatre and Talawa on projects created for young people. She has also project managed live events and installations at the Tate Modern and Royal Festival Hall. Most recently Joni has worked with Shakespeare's Globe and English Touring Opera. Joni worked with Frantic Assembly last year on the Hymns tour.

Andy Purves Technical Stage Manager

Recent and current projects include: lighting, technical design and scenography for found space dance event Ren-Sa with Array, Edinburgh Fringe 2005; spatial and lighting design for Dreams Come Out to Play for 2-6 year olds with Knavish Speech, Edinburgh Fringe 2005 and Birmingham Rep. February 2006, lighting for A Midsummer Night's Dream for Buxton Opera House in the Devonshire Hospital Dome, Buxton; lighting for Almost Blue (Oxford Samuel Beckett Theatre Trust Award Winner), Riverside Studios, lighting and scenography for A Devilish Exercise on the site of the Rose Theatre for the Rose Theatre Trust; lighting for Home Inverness, National Theatre of Scotland opening event with Scott Graham of Frantic Assembly; production electrics and re-lighting for The Wolves in the Wall with the National Theatre of Scotland and Improbable; lighting and technical design for Outre dance and live music event for Array with Warp Records artists at Brighton Festival and Edinburgh Fringe 2006. Awards for lighting design and technical excellence at the National Student Drama Festival 2005. Holds an MA in lighting design from Central School of Speech and Drama, specialising in lighting for site-specific and movement-based theatre.

Emma Barrow Assistant Stage Manager

Since completing her training at Central School of Speech and Drama, Emma has worked as a freelance Stage Manager all around England. Recent productions include Regent's Park Open Air Theatre 2004 and 2006 Seasons, on the shows A Midsummer Night's Dream, Henry IV Part I, The Taming Of The Shrew, Camelot, The Boyfriend and Babe, the Sheep-Pig. Also, A Few Good Men, (Theatre Royal, Haymarket) Abigail's Party (Hampstead Theatre UK Tour) Losing Louis (Hampstead Theatre and Trafalgar Studios) as well as many more productions at Hampstead Theatre including US and Them, The Maths Tutor, How To Behave, Sunday Father and Love Me Tonight, directed by Kathy Burke. Emma has also worked for companies including the Royal Opera House, Cameron Mackintosh Ltd and Goldsmiths University. This is the first time she has worked with Frantic Assembly.

'The indefatigably inventive Frantic Assembly ' Daily Telegraph

Frantic Assembly produces thrilling, energetic and uncompromising theatre. The company is committed to making work that reflects contemporary culture and attracts new audiences to the theatre. In collaboration with a wide variety of artists, Frantic Assembly creates new work that places equal emphasis on movement, design, music and text.

Since its formation in 1992, Frantic Assembly has toured extensively throughout the UK and abroad, building its reputation as one of the country's most exciting companies. Frantic Assembly has collaborated with some of the UK's best contemporary writers including Abi Morgan, Michael Wynne and Mark Ravenhill. Their most recent projects include providing choreography for 'Market Boy' at the National Theatre, the 10th anniversary tour of 'Hymns' and creating the site-specific piece 'Dirty Wonderland' for the Brighton Festival in 2005.

Frantic Assembly operates a UK-wide Education and Training Programme, introducing over 2000 participants a year to the company's methods of creating theatre, developing their physical performance skills and promoting confidence through achievement.

'Choreographed by Frantic Assembly's Scott Graham and Steven Hoggett... this is one of the most physically fluid productions ever to be put on at the National' **(Market Boy)** **The Observer**

'Frantic Assembly's latest theatrical experience, Dirty Wonderland ... is seedy, perverse and utterly delightful.' **(Dirty Wonderland)** **The Independent ★★★★★**

Scott Graham	Artistic Director	Education Associate	**Neil Bettles**
Steven Hoggett	Artistic Director	Creative Associate	**Georgina Lamb**
Lisa Maguire	Executive Producer	International Associate	**Vicki Middleton**
Laura Sutton	Administrator	Board of Directors:	**Virginia Buckley**
			Ben Chamberlain
		(Chair)	**Jane McMorrow**
			Simon Mellor

www.franticassembly.co.uk

The Drum Theatre Plymouth has become a driving force in the South West and beyond, pioneering new forms of stage writing, physical theatre and other innovative work. As part of the Theatre Royal Plymouth complex, it has taken a leading role in an ongoing national exploration of new ways of producing and seeing theatre. In both 2002 and 2005 the Drum Theatre was nominated for the prestigious Peter Brook Empty Space Award.

The Theatre Royal's Young Company and People's Company have residency in the Drum Theatre, which also hosts extensive community and participation work. The Drum includes in its programme a network of leading national theatre companies – Graeae Theatre Company, ATC, Royal Court, Suspect Culture, Paines Plough, Half Moon, Red Shift Theatre Company, Travelling Light Theatre Company and Kesselofski and Fiske.

The Theatre Royal Plymouth is made up of the Theatre Royal itself and the Drum Theatre, as well as TR2, a new, innovative and award-winning Production and Education Centre housing the theatre-making processes, rehearsal facilities and extensive education, access and development activities.

Apart from fulfilling a long held ambition to present in Plymouth a new work by Mark Ravenhill, this premiere of 'pool (no water)' has given us the opportunity to collaborate once again with our friends and colleagues, Scott and Steven of Frantic Assembly. They've been playing the Drum Theatre at least annually for the past decade and have built a dedicated following in the South West.

The Drum's development as an adventurous playhouse has gone hand in hand with Frantics' swift rise as one of the most innovative and talented companies in Europe and they have been a central component both of our programme and of our creative debate.

We have long pioneered collaboration and co-production with partners nationwide, not only to stretch and develop national resources, but more particularly to continue to engage in the swapping of creative ideas and the support of artistic energy wherever it may be found. Happily, in the Lyric Hammersmith, under David Farr and Jessica Hepburn, we have found partners of unusual dynamism and creative clarity.

Simon Stokes, Artistic Director
Theatre Royal Plymouth

Recent productions and co-productions

July 2004	**The Owl Service** adapted by Anita Sullivan and David Prescott from the novel by Alan Garner. **Producer:** Drum Theatre Plymouth
September 2004	**The Wonderful World of Dissocia** by Anthony Nielson **Producers:** Drum Theatre Plymouth, Edinburgh International Festival, Tron Theatre Glasgow
October 2004	**Through A Cloud** by Jack Shepherd **Producers:** Drum Theatre Plymouth and Birmingham REP
February 2005	**Mercury Fur** by Philip Ridley **Producers:** Drum Theatre Plymouth and Paines Plough
May 2005	**Stoning Mary** by Debbie Tucker Green **Producers:** Drum Theatre Plymouth and Royal Court
September 2005	**A Brief History of Helen of Troy** by Mark Shultz **Producers:** Drum Theatre Plymouth and ATC
October 2005	**Presence** by Doug Lucie **Producer:** Drum Theatre Plymouth
February 2006	**The Escapologist** by Simon Bent **Producers:** Drum Theatre Plymouth, Suspect Culture and Tramway
May 2006	**NHS – The Musical** by Nick Stimson and Jimmy Jewell **Producer:** Drum Theatre Plymouth
June 2006	**Pricked** by Anita Sullivan **Producers:** Drum Theatre Plymouth and Ripple
September 2006	**pool (no water)** by Mark Ravenhill **Producers:** Drum Theatre Plymouth, Frantic Assembly and Lyric Hammersmith
October 2006	**Long Time Dead** by Rona Munro **Producers:** Drum Theatre Plymouth and Paines Plough

Drum Theatre Plymouth
Royal Parade, Plymouth, PL1 2TR
01752 267222
www.theatreroyal.com

Chair	**Councillor Nicky Wildy**	Head of Workshop	**Tony Harvey**
Vice Chair	**Peter Vosper**	Head of Wardrobe	**Dina Hall**
Chief Executive	**Adrian Vinken**	Technical Co-ordinator	**Mark Hawker**
Artistic Director	**Simon Stokes**	Marketing Manager	**Marianne Smith**
Production and		Press Officer	**Anne-Marie Clark**
Technical Director	**Paul Clay**		(01752 230479)
Corporate Services		Sales Manager	**Lynn Fletcher**
Manager	**Paul Renyard**	Finance Manager	**Brenda Buckingham**
Artistic Associate	**David Prescott**	Theatre Manager	**Jack Mellor**
Acting Education and		Catering Manager	**Angela Pawson**
Arts Development Manager	**John Whewell**		
Production Managers	**Nick Soper, David Miller**		

Hammersmith

The Lyric Hammersmith is renowned for creating work that takes theatre in new and bold directions. With two spaces, a 550-seat 19th century classical auditorium and a 110-seat studio, it has worked over the past ten years with some of theatre's most groundbreaking artists including Improbable Theatre, Told by an Idiot, Kneehigh Theatre and Frantic Assembly.

Under the Artistic Directorship of David Farr, the Lyric is expanding its work with pioneering companies and artists to explore more innovative and collaborative approaches to theatre-making involving writers, directors, designers, composers and performers. Its aim is to engage audiences of all ages with contemporary theatre that is unexpected and exhilarating.

Alongside its work on the stage, the Lyric has established itself as a leader in arts education with an extensive Creative Learning programme that reaches over 5,000 people a year. Working with some of the most disadvantaged communities in West London, the Lyric provides opportunities for individuals to access innovative, high quality arts provision and develop their creative, personal, social and educational skills.

The Lyric has had a long-standing relationship with Frantic Assembly – over the years they have developed a large and loyal audience here, and we think of ourselves as their London home.

Here at the Lyric we are committed to working with the best, most groundbreaking theatre-makers in the country today, and we are thrilled to be collaborating with Scott Graham, Steven Hoggett and Mark Ravenhill on pool (no water). The combination of Mark's visceral language and Scott and Steven's exhilarating physicality is taking theatre in new directions, and is exactly what the Lyric is about.

We are also delighted to be working alongside Simon Stokes and the Drum Theatre Plymouth, who share the Lyric's commitment to creative innovation and excellence.

David Farr, Artistic Director
Lyric Hammersmith

Lyric
Hammersmith

Artistic Director **David Farr**
Executive Director **Jessica Hepburn**
Producers **Kate McGrath and Louise Blackwell of Fuel**
Head of Finance **Kerrie Smith**
Head of Marketing and Sales **Antonia Seymour**
Co-Directors, Creative Learning **David Baker and James Blackman**
Production Manager **Seamus Benson**
Head of Operations **Damian Ball**

Lyric Board

Chair **Sandy Orr**
Directors **Adjoa Andoh, Cllr Victoria Brocklebank-Fowler,**
Cllr Antony Lillis, Timothy Lloyd Hughes,
Kevin McGrath, Cllr Lisa Nandy, Carol Olivier,
Harbhajan Purewal, Cllr Francis Stainton

The Lyric would like to thank all those who have supported us including
many individuals, trusts and foundations and companies.

Address **Lyric Hammersmith,**
Lyric Square,
King Street,
London W6 0QL

Telephone **08700 500 511**
Web **www.lyric.co.uk**
Email **enquiries@lyric.co.uk**
Fax **020 8741 5965**

supported by
h&f
hammersmith & fulham

Lyric Hammersmith is a Registered Charity No. **278518**

Artistic Directors Note

For the most part Frantic Assembly exists in a generous, supportive and affirming creative community. How thrilling then, to spend an entire creative period considering 'the most dreadfully involuntary of all sins.' Openly discussing artistic jealousy is a compulsive and exhilarating pursuit. Even the most innocuous question, *So, what do you really think of (insert director/show/company here)?* can result in breathtaking displays of vitriol and bile.

What becomes clear almost immediately is just how very human in feels. Not unusual, not painful and, if we are being honest, in the right environment, not that wrong!

To this end Mark brings out the very best and the very worst in us. We only hope we prove to have the same effect on him. His opening line on our first meeting ('Oh, look, it's the Ant and Dec of theatre') was an audacious one but the perfect indication of how things would be - bold, wicked, and very, very funny. But also daring.

Come on, admit it. You hate it when your friends are successful. Or are we on our own? Either way we hope you enjoy us unashamedly addressing our darker side.

Writers note

Some plays just pop into your head and you write them down and then later think about how they might be produced. Other plays – like the ones in this volume – grow out of specific relationships.

I already knew the work of Frantic Assembly and over a couple of years discussed ideas with Steven Hoggett and Scott Graham. We tried out many of our ideas at the National Theatre. POOL (NO WATER) was the eventual result. To all of those who helped us along the way many, many thanks.

CITIZENSHIP grew out of my relationship with the excellent Connections team at the National Theatre, who every year commission ten new plays for young people to perform. I'd already written one of these – TOTALLY OVER YOU – and for the writing of this second play drew as I did for the previous one partly on my own memories of schooldays but also partly on observations of today's young people. I was set right on some matters of contemporary youth speak by members of the National's Young Company, led by Anthony Banks.

pool (no water)

A pool, she had a pool.

Of all of us the most – at least in the eyes of this so-called world – the most successful of us.

So – a pool.

Did she mean to impress? Was it for show?

No. I can't think. No. Because she's . . .

She's good. She's nice. She has integrity. Her roots.

And she has a pool now – it's fantastic fantastic fantastic fantastic.

But she hasn't forgotten us. Visits to rehab. Visits to hospices. Visits to Aids wards. She's made them.

And she comes to our exhibitions. Cramped little exhibitions in lofts in the bohemian quarter. Our photos, our *objets trouvés*, she comes, she sees, she sometimes buys. And she'll help our fund-raising drives.

She's tireless in her help for our fund-raising drives.

We adore her. We adore her. We all absolutely adore her.

Years ago when she was in – when she was in the Group. Life and soul. And she'd always be ripping her clothes off, just ripping them off, and we'd all rip them off too – we'd follow her – and then we'd all make performance pieces or arthouse shorts or we'd just go skinny-dipping for the sheer naked fun of it.

But nowadays she's . . . absent.

Exactly. She's . . . absent. It's that quality in her work that sells. The pieces that first began when we lost Ray to the whole Aids thing. And she used Ray's blood and bandages and catheter and condoms. Pieces that sold to every major collector in the world.

Aha.

Absent. And yet somehow – recognised by the world.

Aha.

And now she has: the pool. The pooooooooool.

First seen in attachments. A Christmas attachment. Open the attachment for a PDF of my new pool.

I open with caution. I have a fear of viruses.

Her pool. 'You're welcome at any time. Come over, share the pool. Any of you – singularly or together – just come over and enjoy the pool.'

And there's the PDF. There's the pool. Clean and blue and lit by beautiful lights. And there's the pool boy – who could have been a porn star. Or maybe is a porn star. Or will be a porn star. And there's her personal trainer taking her through her lengths. And he's a porn star too. And maybe the pool boy fucks the trainer. Or the trainer fucks her. Or she fucks the pool boy.

No no no no – she's always been a very moral person. She's always had a strict code of morals. Even in the hovel days. She never did the hah-hah-heroin for more than a day. And she always kept her door strictly shut at night.

And so we email each other back and forth: yes, let's go and see the pool, let's go and share the pool, why not? Why not? Let's share it with her.

And we email her back. We're coming, we're coming, we're all coming. We're all getting on a plane and coming over to share the pool with you.

And she Es back: Fantastic. Fantastic. Fantastic.

Time drifts, of course. We're all busy – there's exhibitions in the bohemian quarter, there's a project to provide murals for heroin babies, there's fund-raising there's –

There's Sally in the hospice. Sally in that fucking hospice. It's got into her bones now, it's eaten through her body and now that little evil cunting C is eating into her bones – it's got a taste of marrow – and she lies there and she says:

I want to die I want to die all I want is to die why can't they just let I won't take the medication when all I want is to die?

And we say to her

Think of the pool. Think of the pool. That's something to keep going for. We'll get you out of here and fly you out to the pool. Fantastic healing healthy happy times ahead at the pool.

And she says

Yes.

But that's just to humour us. Nobody believes that.

And Sally turns green and Sally turns grey and there's a drip drip drip stuck everywhere and nurses and nuns and we organise a rota because life must go on with its exhibitions and its fund-raising and we take it in turns until we all rush there one night and some of us make it and some of us don't and that's Sally done for.

And you're just stripped naked because suddenly all the art was worth nothing, it is nothing, it means nothing. Sally has gone and Art did nothing and Art could do nothing and Death is big and we are small and really we're nothing, we're nothing.

And *she's* there at the crematorium. And she says: Thank you for looking after Sally. Thank you for that. You were all amazing for looking after. I'm so guilty. I should have been here sooner. And we're: no no no no no.

But I felt did you feel, listen I felt, this is wrong I know this is wrong but I felt, maybe it's only – did anyone else feel – and it is only a feeling, but a feeling is a feeling and I think that should be honoured, you know? If you know what I'm saying? Okay, okay, I'm going to say it, I'm going to tell you, I'm going to tell you what I what I felt, standing in the crematorium and suddenly she's there with her Manager or whoever the, she's there and I want to scream at her: Cunt.

God.

Yes, just open my lungs and scream at her: 'Cunt. Cunt – this is your doing. You did this. You see this casket? You see this casket, see this cheap horrible wooden casket with our friend Sally in it? You did that. That was you.'

God.

'It was you who killed Sally.'

God.

'Because none of us was meant to be wealthy, none of us was meant to be recognised, none of us was meant to fly. We're the Group. And there's balance. And you took away the balance. One of us goes up, then one of us goes down. It's a natural law. Don't you understand the most basic natural law? Well of course you do – understood it and ignored it – on purpose – and killed Sally. Chose to kill Sally. Cunt. Cunt. Cunt.' And if I could I would have torn her hair from her head and torn the clothes from her body and spat into her cunt right then and right there. That was what I . . . Did anyone else . . . ?

No no no no one else. I see. I see. I see.

You see, what bad people. We are all bad people. It needn't be that way of course. No. It needn't. If only we'd use our Art for some good. But instead we harbour . . .

And I think maybe have always harboured, you know right since the hovel, harboured . . .

Now we reflect . . .

Isn't that strange? All the time she was amongst us as a friend, all that time and yet really we harboured the most awful . . . well I suppose *hatred*

Murderous hatred

Would be the only word.

Well that's awful. That is truly terrible.

Yes it is – and we must let that go. We must. Both with our work with the heroin babies, but also in our attitude to her. We must embrace her. We must love her. We must move forward and let go of the past and let go of the badness and move forward with our love for her.

'You're all wiped out,' she says. 'You're all exhausted,' she says.

'Physically and spiritually and emotion. Please come out to the pool. Please. Please. Come on. It's the least I can do.'

And so we all say: yes.

Oh let's leave hatred let's leave death let's leave that behind. The poooooool.

And we go.

It takes so many hours to fly to this strange new world and there are palm trees and heat haze in the dusk of the airport.

And she's there:

Welcome welcome welcome.

And in the huge hallway of the house there's the pool boy and the personal trainer and the cook:

Hello. Hey. Hi. Welcome. Good to. Yeah. How ya? Come on make yourselves anything I can? Fantastic. So you're? Heard so much. That's good.

And yes – we feel a little guilty when we think of all the suffering back in the city – the beatings and the orphan and the pain – and for a moment we want to rush back there and make some art. But we take a moment, take a moment to let that pass – because really are we responsible for every baby whose mother is a junkie? That would be vanity.

And we look at her and we see . . . Yes, really you're just a person. A person like us. And – why did we feel those terrible things all these years? Oh, it feels good to have let them go. And we notice how graceful her movements are and how beautiful her laugh sounds and we actually rather adore the way she's not so present – so pushing herself at you – so *there* as other people are.

And we each of us hold her and say: 'It's good to be here. It's great to see you.' And we actually mean it. And we are lighter than we have been for years.

You know she's a marvellous person. One of us, out in the world and doing well. It's time to celebrate that.

And that night there's a meal – swordfish and watercress and cool cool wine and we get reminiscent and we get cosy and we get tearful. About the – God, do you remember when we are all together when it all seemed to mean so much when everything was so full of meaning yes it was all drenched in meaning and we all cared we all cared so so passionately? Do you remember do you remember do you remember do you remember do you remember the days? Ah yes happy happy happy happy happy happy happy days.

I remember . . . very bright colours. In the crib. In the school. In that first studio we shared. I remember everything having so much colour that I felt: 'God, how can I ever find a medium that has so much colour?'

Time for bed.

And each of us is in a bed.

But suddenly she's there, suddenly her head is round the door:

'I know we said sleep but I thought skinny-dipping let's come on skinny-dipping in the pool before bed.'

God she hasn't lost it despite everything despite all this grandeur she's still . . . naughty naughty naughty.

Magic words from long ago: sk-iii-nn-eeee-dippp-pinnnggg. And we're back out into the night and we're giggling and we're drunk and there's no light in the grounds there's no light on the pool everything's been switched off. And we say: clothes off. Because isn't that the naughtiest, most alive, most wonderful . . . ? Clothes off.

And we take off our clothes.

And each of us knows that our body is not what it was those ten years before – that there's sag and fat and lines even and even even the littlest hints of grey. Oh yes the sad sad rot to the grave has already begun.

But that doesn't matter in the darkness. In the darkness we're as we were ten years ago when we strip poker and performance pieces and all that naked fun.

And it's just so beautiful. Slightest breeze around your cracks, hanging a little in the wind.

And some of us cry and some of us laugh but we're all moved by the sheer naked beauty of it.

I'll always remember that moment, always. Just something . . . all of us standing there naked in the dark. Sometimes now when the painkillers aren't working I try to visualise that moment and then things don't seem so awful.

Come on she squeals come on the pool!

And then she's running and whooping through the darkness and she launches herself and you can just see her up in the sky, up against the sky, the arc of her body through the night sky up and up and up and up.

She seems so high. She's flying. She's an angel. A drunken laughing goddess angel.

And then she arcs down and we're clapping and we're cheering.

And then

Some of us thought we heard the splash. You do. When you think there's going to be a splash then you hear a splash. You do the work. But we didn't hear the splash. There was no splash. There was

The crack

The cracking of her body.

The harsh crack of her body against the concrete.

Then there was silence.

Then there was her groan and her squeal and her screams of pain.

Aaaaaaggghooooowooooooowooowwwwwwww.

We edge forward in the darkness our naked figures moving forward in the dark until we're at the edge at the pool. And then we see, see as our eyes adjust

Pool. No water.

Just hints of water in a pool now drained.

And there in the middle of the concrete her body twisted and crunched and crushed and her noise now animal no more of god or angel. Ooooaaaaaawwwww.

We don't speak. We don't look at each other. We're too together now to need to look or speak to each other at all.

And we climb down and we climb down into the pool.

And we stand around her.

She was still conscious then. Still screaming and crying and jerking.

And we wanted to feel what she was feeling – she is one of us, we are artists – no, we're people – we wanted to feel what she was feeling – share the pain.

But it didn't happen.

We stood. We stood and we watched the jerking and we heard the screams. And we stood and we watched. All of us.

We couldn't do anything. Couldn't touch her. But we could have felt something. A life without empathy is . . .

She didn't jerk for long. She . . . went. Did she die? I suppose for a moment it crossed my mind and I was – no she didn't die and I think somehow we knew she didn't die. She 'passed from consciousness'.

And the great absent thing is lying at our feet and we're thinking:

This is right. This feels – there is right in that.

I'm sorry you had to suffer, I'm sorry there's this pain – but there is justice in this. Something is shaping our ends.

For Sally, for Ray, for us, this had to be.

You see you flew – yes – you reached out your wings and you flew above us. And that's okay. You tried and congratulations.

For trying. But you thought that could last? Flying above the ground, looking down on our lives in the city below? You really thought that could last? Of course that couldn't last. And now you've crashed right down. And that hurts doesn't it? I understand. That hurts.

This feels good. This feels wonderful. Look at you. Hah. Hah. Just look at you. I am great.

There is strength in me. Oh the strength in me I never knew I had.

You bitch you bitch you bitch you bitch you bitch you bitch you bitch.

And we

Maybe you will die. Maybe death will come for you. And if it's come for you, it hasn't come for me. That's me saved for another day.

And we

You shit you shit you evil evil evil evil shit to think these things of another person what kind of evil lies inside you?

And we

You've patronised my. You've patronised my exhibitions in the bohemian quarter. At last at last I can patronise you. I can care. What better way to patronise you back than care for this mangled crippled body?

And her face. You would have thought – locked into a grimace of pain, intense emotion. But no – her face on top of that crunched-up body her face was as absent as it had ever been. And if I could have drilled into her skull – or ripped it off – just to know what thoughts and feelings went through her head, then I would. I swear to God, I would.

There's a little stream of piss comes out of her now – green from all the wine. And it's the – funny to think of it now – it's the piss that focuses our minds.

And we organise and we call and we open doors and we're –
you go in the ambulance I'll follow in a –

Oh please take care of my friend. Please. The most awful
accident. Please.

As in that room she's wired up and dripped up and hooked up
and we come and go and bring each other coffee and cigarettes
and we pace the corridors and we ask the doctors and the
nurses for news news news any news? We would never dare
tell each other just how – and this is the word – exciting this is.

Did you feel that – ? I wish there was something else but there
was –

The excitement that all of us deny. Because excitement is not –
no, not an appropriate response.

'It's touch and go with your friend,' the doctor tells us. 'It's
distinctly touch and go.'

Come on you cunt feel oh feel oh – but we look – we look like
we're supposed to look, we do the – the little tilt of the head,
the little sigh, the tear comes down the cheek – just like we
know it should.

Her body – her body is broken in our head. A picture but not –
it's not a feeling you know? And you would have thought
above all else an artist would –

And in the room one of us or all of us – anyway somebody
says to her:

'You can't hear but I have felt the most awful things towards
you. And that won't continue. It can't continue. You are down
and I am going to care for you. Please let me in and I will love
you. Don't be absent. Be here. Please.'

And back in her house we lay our heads down and we see them
parading through our room – Sally with her breast eaten away,
Ray with a lung no bigger than a matchbox and now this – and
we want to join the parade and march down to hell or heaven
or purgatory but we don't because we have a diazepam and a
smoke, a wine and a diazepam – and that's okay.

The next day the personal trainer sobs. The cook howls. The pool boy threatens an overdose. The boy who drained the pool without notice the boy who – We console them. We are all benificence. We discover – oh wonderful – what good people we are.

And of course as soon as we humanly can we go to the hospital.

We can't remember now. It doesn't matter. Oh of course it matters to curators it matters to historians . But to us it doesn't matter at all. But one of us first thought of taking a camera.

We don't even know who first packed the digi-digi-digi-digi-cam for our visit. Maybe we all did. Maybe each of us did. Maybe each of us spontaneously came to that same conclusion. Yes – maybe each of us knew that an image, a record, a frame – maybe we all knew that was the thing to do.

But there we are – hospital with the camera in our hand.

And we're here. We're here. We're here in the room with the camera and the sunlight coming through the blinds.

Hello. Hello. It's us.

Please wake and stop us. Don't let us do that. You don't have to burble on. Just open your eyes. That's all. Do you know how much we used to – you were just so much a part of us and now . . .

And we hold the camera down by our sides.

Come on. Just look. And see. And feel. And care. It's a natural human thing. But we . . .

And you see now – look – what it's done to her. Now the blood's been cleaned away. The body bruised and swollen into shape no other human's yet achieved. Her limbs in plastic. Her neck in plastic. Her mask. The drips and the tubes. And the machines that inhalate and beeeep. A moving . . . a timeless picture of the . . .

Our friend yes but also . . .

The line of the machine . . .

The purple of the bruise . . .

It appeals. It tempts. There is beauty here. We know, we've spent our life hunting it out and there is beauty here.

And we stand and we look and at last we're moved by the intense beauty of that image.

(Throw camera – disgusting thing – through window and eight floors to the street below.)

If you'd been in that room with us then maybe, maybe you'd have felt the same. Because today we are all artists.

And the light was good and the potential for composition was all there – and to be honest it was easy easy easy easy to come up with those images that so later seemed striking.

(Stamp on that lens and shit on that viewfinder and tear the memory out by the soul.)

And the temptation to arrange – just to move the bed . . . so . . . so the composition was . . . get her head in the light, so. The temptation was great and we were weak. So we wheel her into light and actually move the limbs and head – checking of course not to disrupt the tubes and drips and . . . science and art can work together happily.

It took a few moments to snap.

And it felt –

Later, we sat in the smoking room and said to ourselves:

That wasn't a good thing to do. That was a terrible thing to do. Why not select delete and wipe away what you've . . . ? Why not?

And we did. No – honest with you – we nearly did. But we never did.

And that night on the laptop we survey our work and we – ah – we are not disgusted with ourselves as we expect we should. We are already thinking interviews – exhibition – catalogue – sale.

The next two months. The daily round.

The morning to the hospital wait for your chance collect your images while you can.

Oh how well we get to know that hospital! And for a while I actually dated the nurse – Miguel – we had blood tests to check for infections and confided the results but I wasn't ready to commit so that ended. And I think Miguel might actually have suspected – there were some questions – about the daily photos. Not that there was anything wrong . . .

Still we were furtive for that whole time. Maybe just for the thrill . . .

Then evenings back to survey what we've done.

Start to arrange, start to order, start to catalogue. Start to – print with a quality of drenched colour, tone and definition and . . .

Her home is our home, our studio. And in the morning the sun rises on us and at nights the sprinklers bless the lawn and we are fed and attended to by her staff.

And my body – during that time my body starts to rise and tauten as the trainer comes at six and we run through the suburbs to that gym and in the afternoon I swim fifty lengths in the pool.

I wish I'd had a nutritionist before. I feel fabulous.

And in time – the right dealer, the right agent, the right publicist – this will be an important series of images.

We've become fascinated by the – look you can see – fascinated by the way the markings and the bruisings and the cuts progress from day to day.

Just look. Just look. Just look and see. Isn't that rather interesting? Isn't that fascinating?

The way the bruises and the swellings grow and ripen over her. The myriad colours that a bruise can take. One day an eye revealed and then another concealed beneath the swollen. Yes.

And we feel together. We feel as one. There is a job of work to do and we are doing it.

Oh we are alive − would you look at that, the old corpse is back from the brink − and I'm shaking a stump and I'm walking the earth and I'm breathing the air.

Hurrah! Hurrah! Hurrah!

Don't sing it too loud but

Hurrah! Hurrah! Hurrah!

Join me if you will

Hurrah! Hurrah! Hurrah!

We're the Group! We're the Group! We're the Group!

But happiness is . . . Happiness is so fast. Eight weeks and then . . .

We arrive as usual. And Miguel − we weren't dating by now that had finished some ooo − Miguel comes forward and he is smiling at us. Beaming.

And we know, we know. We can say the words for him.

'Your friend is conscious.'

Oh.

Two months and Sleeping Beauty is . . .

Oh.

And I felt light because . . . because that had been . . . what was that − ? Taking those images? Snatching that . . . ? No no no no. That wasn't a thing that we were supposed to do. That was a . . . oh relief relief. This is . . . saved.

'That is wonderful.'

I am so happy that art has gone away and now we can be people.

Let her be present. Please. Let her be . . .

I did a line before I went into her room. I never told anybody that before. I knew I had just enough for a line and in the nappy-changing facility I . . . I don't understand myself.

'Hello. Look it's us. We're all here.'

She's not awake – not awake like you and me – she's slipping in and out – but sometimes her eyes open and she'll look at us and she sees us. She's in the room with us. once she even gives us her smile. I swear to God.

And we're happy. For her. But also for us. A quiet happy but still . . .

And we talk that hospital talk that burble that you talk to the semi-conscious and to babies. We burble a nice sound because she deserves the sweetest baby talk.

'We're going to go skinny-dipping. Any day now. That's what we're gonna do. We're gonna get you out of here. And we're all gonna strip and it's going to be back . . .

. . . You will be one of us just as it was all the decade past everything stripped away and us just a bunch of cunts of dicks and titties and bumcracks us the bathing beautiful oh think of that my darling think of. We are so lucky to have known and we'll know it again. We will. We will. We will.'

I kiss her. She doesn't do anything. But that's okay. Everything is . . .

And we say to each other: It's over. She's mending. Happy days are coming.

And we hold hands and we smile and we hug and we sing. The Group stand around her bed and we sing and she opens her eyes and she looks at us and . . .

I think for a moment . . . no.

Yes I thought . . . I don't know whether anyone else thought . . .

Maybe all of us thought . . .

She knows. She knows what we have been doing. She sees the camera in our pocket and she understands. How much wiser than us she is.

But that couldn't be.

So we hold the water to her lips and we stroke her fingers and we breathe:

We love you.

And she says:

Thank you for being my friends through all of these years.

And – no – she didn't know that thoughts of hate had ever gone through our heads and we are – well – blessed – and – um – absolved by those words. And that feels very good.

And for hours we are there with her as she sleeps and wakes and I think this was the . . . calmest I have ever been in my life.

So why – back at her house did we start to – ? I let the gym slip those weeks. My belly sags.

I drive-thru and the chicken wings and ice cream until my stomach burns.

One night with lots of wine and spliff and cokeycokeycoke an actual row. Subject – nothing. But screaming and slamming and tears and silence.

And actually you know it's at moments like this that I find that my depepependcy issues really emerge? Because I want to – oh Counsellor – I want to be part of the Group that's what I want so much but if they won't maybe I've excluded mmmm ah shit there's no fucking needles in this fucking room what's a hospital room without a needle you know?

And the – I'll give you a hundred to sleep with me. Leave the pool for a moment. Leave the pool alone just for one goddam minute and give me one good fuck won't you? What is wrong with my money?

And Ray and Tommy and Sally are rattling around in my room. Call it a drug-abuse-related issue if you like. But I call it grief when the bones of dead friends are banging against your head and drowning out the sounds of life, while we . . . Eat. Sleep. Shit. Wank. Begin again. Eat. Sleep. Shit. Wank. Begin again.

Oh yes. That's right. One of us decided to show her the images. Well – I can't remember which . . .

I don't think it was me but . . .

Maybe I could have . . .

Anyway one of us – we were – what? – all in the room and there was something about her smile then, the way she looked at us as we cared for her.

I felt like she was accusing me and I . . .

It's so hard to know what she's thinking. Always been like that. But normally you feel like she's . . . judging.

And I just wanted . . .

Somebody thought: I have to tell her. To make myself feel better.

Maybe to hurt her.

And she was looking down at her body – still purple and twisted – and she says:

'No mirror anywhere. I must look like shit. I guess they don't want me to see what . . .'

And there was a voice:

'Oh you can see what you look like.'

'Yes?'

'But maybe you shouldn't. Maybe it's best.'

'No. I'd like to see.'

She didn't stop us you see, there was every chance.

'You've got a mirror?'

'No but . . . '

The laptop out. That first week in the hospital. She's barely human. Scroll. Week two, three, on through the months. She begins to heal.

And she's watching. But I couldn't see . . .

Still nothing in her eyes.

And then she asks:

'Where do these come from?'

And so we:

We took them.

And I thought she'd understand the evil inside us. But I really don't think she did because anyway she says:

'Thank you.'

Like she means it.

She didn't want us to put the laptop away. But we did. The battery was running flat.

And then she says:

'Can you take me to the toilet?'

They'd removed her catheter by then and so I supported her to the toilet and I felt okay because I was holding her and she really needed me.

And you know there were visits when she didn't mention the images. I don't know – three? four? – several visits when they didn't come up.

In my mind several weeks when they were unspoken. And I suppose actually it wasn't wrong, it was – what's the word? – kind to record that for her.

Well yes, if we'd done it for her. Yes. And if we hadn't arranged the body. Planned the exhibition. If we could forget.

And then one day she says:

'Bring the camera.'

'Oh . . . no.'

'Yes. Bring the camera. I want to carry on. I'm still healing. I'm getting stronger all the time. And I'd like to carry on recording that.'

What could we do but bring the camera?

She laughed that day. She was so happy. She turned her head into the light to show the bruise. She pulled up the gown to show the wounds, the stitches, the bone almost sticking through the blue flesh.

She is driven by an energy we haven't seen for years.

'You stand over there. Here – get the drip in the frame beside the cuts on the hand.'

And we carry out her commands. So many images and then:

'Let me see let me see let me see myself.'

It's an order. Delivered like a child but still . . .

And so we scroll through and she studies intently and oh . . .

That's the kind of moment when any sane person needs a K hole you know? Just to get you out of that room.

And she likes them.

And all that energy.

Every day she drives us on. And every day is recording her.

The old routine was naughty. She was sleeping. We were snatching bits of her. And now . . .

It is our job to make her happy. And she loves this. And she grows stronger every day. While we . . . we actually started to feel rather sickly you know?

I have headaches. I have migraines. This morning I slipped while shaving and see the see the cut. No it's alright but yes yes actually it does actually sting. But you mustn't worry about me.

Doctor doctor I think the pool boy may have passed on something fungal. I'm yeasty and I want to cry about it.

We want her to sleep. We don't want her to tire herself. She should be sleeping all the time but now . . . we are the exhausted ones. The visits to the hospital. The fluorescent light. That bad coffee. It is very tiring.

And now she wants hard copies. So we provide hard copies.

And she lays them out around the room, arranges, rearranges, studies. And – yes – sometimes she does ask our opinions but really it is her eye, her eye shaping them into a form.

She is so good at what she does. She has shown at such fantastic galleries. You actually learn from her working her way through those images. Which is a privilege.

But we still have to take her to the toilet. Remember. At the end of the day . . . we still have to take her to the toilet.

It had never crossed our mind that she might have other visitors so when we saw . . .

Tall. Rich. Tanned. Bit of a cunt.

'Who was he?'

'He owns the gallery that I work with out here. We've been talking about the work I want to show when I get out of here.'

What work?

'Oh . . . just ideas.'

But I knew. It was lost then. It was her body. She had dived into the pool. It was her act. And we thought we took the images but she was the work. And she has everything and we have – oh – nothing.

I can't do this any fucking longer you know? Give me a break. Let me succeed.

She would claim the images and we would be back in the bohemian quarter doing – oh – very good work with the underprivileged. But be honest – I've done my dues – I want to be privileged.

And now it feels like punishment to take those daily images of her. You can hear what will be said about her. You know who will buy these.

I must do something else with my life. But what?

So have a party in her room. Spliff away. Let's feel as though we're all together in this and making these pictures. Let's really do everything we can to feel that.

And now the time comes. It's winter. She's coming home.

Excitement. Something we can organise.

She's made a list of course. Clothes and make-up that we have to take to prepare her. In we go. She's sitting on the bed, expectant, ready now to go. Clothes on with some assistance make-up artfully applied.

And walking through the ward she looks so strong so well. Amongst the injured dying lines she looks so strong as if to insult each of them one by one. And it's us following behind who look the weaker. The weak ones stepping in her step.

But on the street – where the healthy ones parade around and flirt and deal and hustle and threaten – well there – even as she passes through the revolving door and into the rain – suddenly she seems the weaker. Suddenly you see the way her limbs are now not set quite right, the drag and hobble of her frame. You see the way no make-up known can quite conceal the swollen face. Just one step from hospital to street – but all the difference. And she's the stranger here. This is our world – despite the shabby little lives we've led – this is our world and she's not quite finding her feet.

And we are good again. We are good. As we help her into taxi, give directions, hold her as a bump or turn inflicts a little pain upon her. We're here for you, we're guiding you, we love you. We're taking you through the darkness. Trust us. Love us. Please.

She's tired at home. She takes in banners cakes the pool. A little smile. That little smile she's always given year on year and never given anything away. The smile that you can make of what you will. But the smile done she's dozing and we say:

Come on to bed to bed to rest that's what you need it's all so much you need to rest.

And we watch over her and we do care for her. We do genuinely – it's very important that you should believe this bit – we do genuinely care.

There's interrupted sleep. She's seeing it again and again when her eyes are shut. Slipping off the clothes. The leap into the air. The arc up and up into the stars. Swoop down. And then the instant of concrete. The instant of knowledge of all the pain that must come and then – crack. And she's awake.

But we're there. There's always one of us there. And she smiles and says

Thank you thank you thank you thank you for being here.

And we say:

Silly you silly no we want to be here.

And it's true. We do. We really do.

And she has visitors. Her manager. Her publicist. The gallery owner.

And we welcome them and we show them up to her room.

And we smile at them and offer them drinks and we can't make out the words of the conversation that is going on above our heads.

But really we know. We know that this story. Her story. The pictures. This is what they are dealing in. Selling. Packaging. Promoting. Launching. They are getting ready for the launch day.

And we are housemaids really and any day now we'll be deported home.

And look honestly years ago who would have thought . . . ? She was the least of us honestly.

Then one day she

Let's get out the images. Let's put them out around the room.

Here we go. Here we go. She's preparing. So we . . .

No no you're not ready you're not ready for that not while you're getting better no not now later we can go through them.

Promise?

Of course of course we promise you.

And that was meant. We meant it then. Nothing hidden then.

I wouldn't say the virus was willed. It wasn't quite as clear as that. No one of us actually sat down and said

Come you virus come enter in my inbox spread your stain through modem into memory and mainframe come.

That would be ridiculous. But I do think one of us in our heart of wretched hearts knew that the attachment was a dupe, knew that opening 'read me' would wreck the laptop file by file, taking out the images – zap zappy zappy zap.

We protested

Shit shit shit

But we hadn't backed up so . . . something going on more than just a freak.

Didn't tell her. Kept on

Rest now and when you're then the images yes yes yes.

And we hadn't lost them all. The bulk had but there were some still in the camera memory a few hard copies left. Enough to piece together even if – even if – even if –

Well even if chunks of – great big chunks of actually – whole chapters of – some key bits of the – even if 'read me' had actually fucked up the story of her healing so now she healed in leaps and starts – a nonsense narrative.

But there was a kind of – still enough to satisfy her need no doubt.

And the day was coming. The day was coming now. The day when we had promised her that she could see the images laid out from the first stolen shots of her swollen mangled totally unconscious frame right through to those final few days – the final rush of wellness in the hospital.

Tomorrow we tell her tomorrow. Tomorrow you will come down and it will all be presented in the living room – the gallery of you.

Thank you

She says and off she drifts sleeping with the calmest smile you've ever seen.

And we sit in silence. Waiting for . . .

Oh God.

Waiting for . . .

I blame the personal trainer. He wouldn't be the first – is there a personal trainer in this world who doesn't deal as well as train? But it was the personal trainer who dealt us the stuff that night. He was selling but yes okay and we were buying.

I thought I was clean I really thought I was so clean. But I'm not. I never am. Never will be. I'm a user and I always will be. Until the day I die. Isn't that great? Isn't it fucking great? Because I know who I am. This is me. I'm a userjunkiecunt-crackwhorefeelmyKholecuntedtwat that's me and it feels . . . fucking great.

I am alive I am alive. Sober is dead. The faces of the fucking sober dead and I am so fucking from my cunt to my arse to my tits to my mouth I am fucking alive.

Kiss me kiss me somebody stick a tongue in me or up me or I don't fucking care come on humans let's human each other or sniff cracks I don't care let's be human isn't that great with the this is are you up? I'm up and up and up and up and cunted and cunted and c-c-c-c-cunted. Woah! There's no fucking coming down now.

Turn the music up turn the music up turn the music up turn
the music up I want my stomach to bleeeeeeeeeed when you
turn the music up.

And then one of us produced the camera, produced the
memory. Choose our first image and

Delete

Oh yes oh yes oh yes oh yes oh yes.

And then a great wave of fun

Select Delete Select Delete Select Delete Select Delete Select
Delete Select Delete Select Delete Select Delete Select Delete
Select Delete Select Delete Select Delete Select Delete Select
Delete Select Delete Select Delete Select Delete Select Delete
Select Delete Select Delete Select Delete Select Delete Select
Delete Select Delete Select Delete Select Delete Select Delete
Select Delete Select Delete Select Delete Select Delete Select
Delete Select Delete Select Delete Select Delete Select Delete
Select Delete Select Delete Select Delete Select Delete Select
Delete Select Delete Select Delete Select Delete Select Delete
Select Delete Select Delete Select Delete

Until not a single memory of the 'miracle of healing' left.

A little pause then as we drunk in what we'd done. A little
chance to celebrate how strong we are now. God – the triumph
pumping through our torsos.

But look . . . there's the hard copies. Yes the hard copies. The
last remaining bit.

Let's stop now. It's done now. We know we are strong. We
know it.

I'm coming down. Look at me. I'm coming down actually.
Fuck I need water.

Oh no we're up now. Please let's . . . please don't let this end.

This is the only thing we will ever do on this planet and we
know that. Our lives are nothing. Our work is nothing. No be
honest with ourselves fucksake our work is nothing.

And our work is nothing and we are no people. We have ruined our lives. We took a wrong turning into art and it has taken us nowhere and it's too late now to discover our talent.

And look at our bodies look at them my tits are jjjjjust moving every day towards the grave.

And I wish I had Aids or cancer – Sally lucky Ray lucky – Aids or cancer so I didn't have to suffer the slow drip-drip-drip-indignity of the everyday drag of life.

So – don't turn back now. Don't do that.

Pedro – come back over here and bring as much fucking gear as you've got we'll buy the lot.

Alright my friends alright. This is it. Music please from every speaker. Stick a bit of porn on the plasma and it's . . . chemical roulette . . . whatever you pull out the hat you inject or inhale or you stuff up your arse.

Here we go here here we go here h – h-h-h-h-h-h – here weeee g-g – g-gooooo!

And the lighter – the first flame on the corner of the first image of her healing. We whoop and laugh and are delighted at the flames flaring up and blanking it away.

Taking it in turns now

Let me burn I'm next I'm the next to burn

The bonfire

And we dance we dance about in total free free freedom as the images away in guttering and fumes and blaze.

It's going it's going it's going soon be nothing left.

What's going on?

She's there. Just a T-shirt and she's in the doorway.

What are you doing?

And we want to say:

You know you know you know what we're doing. Surely you know you knew we had to?

But we don't. We stand and watch her. Silence. She's moving in. She takes the centre. And she takes it in. And sees.

And she understands then – she knows.

Everything she thought was friendship was hate. Everything that was care was envy. Concern was destroy. And we hold her in her hands and we have snapped her neck and we have broken her legs and we have trodden on her skull.

And finally. Oh finally she is absent no longer. And her mouth bellows:

'You are small people. You have always been small people. Ever since the day. There are small people and there are big people. And I am a big person and you are not. Yes? Yes? Yes?

'Oh I've held this in all these years but no more.

'I have talent. I have vision. I am blessed. You are not.

'You can graft if you like but that is all it will ever be. Whatever you do none of you can ever touch me.

'You thought I didn't see all your jealousy and hatred all these years? Of course I saw it.

'And Sally and Ray died because they were too weak to live, to live and and make art.

'I am the only one of you strong enough ever to really live and nothing you can do will ever destroy. Because I will always be the stronger.

'So write to me please from time to time and let me know about your small lives.'

And you know when she said it – such a relief that she wasn't absent any more after so many years.

And really – oh really – she spoke the truth.

And so really I suppose it was one of the happiest nights of my life.

No actually it was the happiest night of my life. To have somebody tell you the truth like that . . . try to get somebody to do it to you if you can . . . try it tonight . . . it's really fantastic.

And now. Years have gone. And look at these arms – no track marks – nothing. Clean. And these four here – new teeth. Beauties.

And I actually met someone who I rather like and I have two children – one is two, the other is four – and they like me so that makes it feel rather better. Because when we're all playing around the paddling pool things seem rather okay. And the children have their own little mobile phones – for safety – and they like to take pictures of Mummy lying in the pool. And that's lovely.

And I like to think there's a rehab or an Aids ward or a somewhere where we'll be together once again. Somewhere where we'll meet and be the gang. But – hey I'm a romantic. I'm a foolish old romantic as the years go on.

So. Light the candles. Bake the cake. Sing the song. The gang's all here. We're here together. And the dream is dreamy and oh life is long.

Citizenship

Citizenship was developed by the NT Shell Connections 2005 programme and premiered in the Cottesloe auditorium of the National Theatre, London, in March 2006. The cast was as follows:

Amy	Claire-Louise Cordwell
Tom	Sid Mitchell
Gary	Matt Smith
Ray	Robert Boulter
Stephen	Andrew Garfield
Kerry	Farzana Dua Elahe
Chantel	Andrea Riseborough
Alicia	Naomi Bentley
De Clerk	Richard Dempsey
Melissa	Matti Houghton
Tarot Reader	Joy Richardson
Baby	Alex Tregear
Martin	Javone Prince
Directed by	Anna Mackmin
Designed by	Jonathan Fensom
Lighting by	Jason Taylor
Music by	Paddy Cunneen
Sound Designer	Christopher Shutt

One

Amy, **Tom**.

Amy You got the Nurofen?

Tom Yeah.

Amy Take four.

Tom It says two.

Amy Yeah, but if you're gonna really numb yourself you gotta do four.

Tom I dunno.

Amy Do you want it to hurt?

Tom No.

Amy Then take four. Here.

Amy *passes* **Tom** *vodka. He uses it to wash down four Nurofen.*

Amy Now put the ice cube on your ear.

Tom *does this.*

Amy Now you gotta hold it there till you can't feel nothing.

Tom Thanks for helping

Amy It's gonna look good.

Tom Yeah?

Amy Yeah, really suit you.

Tom Thass good.

Amy You got a nice face.

Tom I don't like my face.

Amy I think it's nice.

Tom Sometimes I look in the mirror and I wish I was dead.

Amy I got rid of mirrors.

Tom   Yeah.

Amy   Mum read this feng shui thing and it said I wasn't supposed to have them. You numb now?

Tom   Almost. You got a nice face.

Amy   You don't have to lie.

Tom   I'm not. You're fit.

Amy   I know I'm plain. But that's okay. I talked to my therapist.

Tom   What did she say?

Amy   That I have to love myself in case nobody else does.

Tom   Your mum loves you.

Amy   I suppose. You ready now?

Tom   I reckon.

Amy *produces a needle.*

Tom   Is that clean?

Amy   I put it in Dettol.

Tom   Alright.

Amy   Let's start.

She starts to push the needle into **Tom***'s ear but he pulls away.*

Amy   I can't do it if you do that.

Tom   I know.

Amy   You gotta sit still.

Tom   Maybe we should leave it. Maybe not today.

Amy   I thought you wanted an earring.

Tom   I know.

Amy   Thass what you been saying for weeks: I wanna earring, I wanna earring.

Tom   I know, only –

Amy   I'll go careful. Come here. You're a baby.

Tom   No.

Amy   I'll treat you nice and soft. Like a baby.

Tom   Alright.

He comes back.

Amy   Bit more vodka.

Tom *drinks.*

Amy   Bit more.

Tom *drinks.*

Amy   Bit more.

Tom *drinks.* **Amy** *pushes the needle into his ear.*

Tom   Aaaagggghhh.

Amy   Thass it.

Tom   It hurts.

Amy   Nearly there.

Tom   Do it quickly. Do it. Aggghhh.

Amy   Soon be finished.

Tom   Right. Right. Is there blood?

Amy   What?

Tom   Is there blood?

Amy   I dunno.

Tom   I can feel blood

Amy   Maybe a bit.

Tom   Shit. Shit. Shit.

Amy   It's not much. You're gonna be alright.

Tom   Yeah. Yeah. Yeah. Yeah. Yeah. Yeah. Yeah.

He faints.

Amy   Tom? Tom! Shit. Shit.

She drinks a lot of vodka.

Tom – please.

Her mobile rings.

(*On phone.*) Kez? No. I'm fucking – I'm having a panic attack.
Like I used to, yeah. Tom's dead. He's died. Just now. Shit.
I killed him. I've killed Tom. I wanna kill myself. Shit.

Tom *groans.*

Amy (*on phone*)   He made a noise. Yeah, well. He came back
to life. I gotta go. Kez – I'm going now.

Tom   Whass going on?

Amy   You sort of went.

Tom   Who's on the phone?

Amy   Thass Kerry. She's getting stressed out cos she's gotta
give the baby back tomorrow.

Tom   Baby?

Amy   Life Skills.

Tom   Oh yeah.

Amy   You remember Life Skills? Each of the girls has gotta
take it in turns to looks after this baby – plastic baby. It puts
you off having a real one. You could have memory loss.

Tom   No.

Amy   Like Shareen after the overdose. Her mum and dad
went to see her in the hospital and she didn't know who they
were.

Tom   I haven't got memory loss.

Amy   Alright.

Tom   Fucking stupid idea letting you do that. I should have
gone to a fucking professional. Fucking go to somebody who
knows what they're fucking doing 'stead of letting you fucking
fuck the whole thing up.

Amy   I was trying to help.

Tom   Yeah, well, you're no help – you're rubbish. You're
total rubbish.

Amy   Don't give me negative messages.

Tom   Trying to kill me with your stupid needle.

Amy   I can't be around people who give me negative
messages.

Tom   I fucking hate you.

Amy   No. I'm sorry. I'm sorry. I'm sorry.

She cries.

Tom   Come on. Don't. No. No.

Amy   I can't do anything right. I'm useless.

Tom   No.

Amy   I am. Thass why I cut myself. Cos I'm totally useless.
Ughhh.

Tom   Hey hey hey.

He holds **Amy**.

Tom   Come on. Alright. Alright. Alright. You better?

Amy   I dunno.

Tom   You're alright. You're a good person. I like you.

Amy   Yeah?

Tom   I really like you.

Amy   Thass good.

Tom   You got a nice face.

Amy *kisses* **Tom**.

Tom   Oh.

Amy   Was that wrong?

Tom   I didn't mean you to do that.

Amy   Oh. Right. Right.

Tom   I didn't wanna kiss you. Only –

Amy   Yeah?

Tom   I'm not ready for . . .

Amy   You're fifteen.

Tom   I know.

Amy   You gotta have done . . .

Tom   No.

Amy   Why?

Tom   It doesn't matter.

Amy   Tell me.

Tom   I have this dream. And in this dream I'm kissing someone. Real kissing. Tongues and that. But I can't see who I'm kissing. I don't know if it's a woman. Or a man. I try to see the face. But I can't.

Amy   Are you gay?

Tom   I don't know.

Amy   There's bisexuals.

Tom   You won't tell anyone?

Amy   No. Are you going to decide?

Tom   What?

Amy   What you are?

Tom   I don't know.

Amy   Or find out?

Tom   I don't know.

Amy   Don't waste yourself, Tom. You've got a nice face.

Tom   Yeah.

Amy *gets a text message.*

Amy   It's Kerry. She says the baby's gone to sleep.

Tom   It's not real.

Amy   It is to her.

Tom   I'm gonna go.

Amy   Finish off the vodka.

Tom   No. Thanks. Forget what I told you.

Amy   You're still bleeding. There's still some –

Tom   I got coursework.

Exit **Tom***.* **Amy** *drinks.*

Two

Gary, **Tom***. They are smoking a joint.*

Tom   Good draw.

Gary   Got it off my mum's boyfriend for my birthday. Ten big fat ones for my fifteenth.

Tom   Thass cool.

Gary   Thass the last. He had a fight with his dealer last night. Dealer come round the house and they had a big barney. An' me mum's ragga CDs got smashed in the ruck.

Tom   Shit.

Gary   Yeah. She is well gutted.

Enter **Ray** *and* **Stephen***.*

Ray   Wass 'appening?

Gary   Chilling.

Ray   You shag Amy last night? We wanna know. You get jiggy?

Stephen   Jiggy-jiggy.

Ray   Is she your bitch? You ride her like your bitch?

Tom   Fuck's sake.

Gary   You got problems.

Ray   What?

Gary   I'm saying: you got problems.

Ray   What you saying? I got problems.

Gary   Yeah, you got problems. No respec'.

Ray   I respec'.

Gary   No respec' for woman.

Ray   I respec' woman.

Gary   Ride her like a bitch? Didn't he say?

Tom   Yeah.

Ray   That's what I said.

Stephen   He said it.

Ray   That's what I said. I ride her *and* respec' woman.

Stephen   Yeah. Ride and respec'.

Ray   You chat shit. What are you? What is he?

Stephen   He is gay.

Gary   All I'm saying –

Ray   So gay. You are so totally gay, Gary.

Gary   Just sayin' –

Ray   You are like the most totally gay person anyone knows.

Gary   I'm not.

Ray   Gay Gary. Thass what you are. Respec'? What are you
chattin'? You're chattin' gay. You are fucking wrong, man.
Wrong in your head. Wrong in your, your . . . hormones, man.
Totally totally wrong.

Gary   Thass not right.

Ray (*to* **Tom**)   Come on, man. Say something. Tell him.

Tom   I . . .

Ray   You're always watching. You're never talking. Tell him.

Tom   Listen, I wanna –

Ray   You fucking tell him.

Stephen   Tell the battyboy.

Ray   You fucking tell him.

Tom   . . . You're gay, Gary.

Gary   Shit.

Tom   Everyone says it. Everyone call you it. Gay Gary.

Gary   I know what they say.

Tom   You shouldn't talk gay.

Stephen   Thass right.

Tom   Cos no one likes a person who talks gay.

Gary   You chat shit, Tom.

Ray   Listen, he's tellin' you –

Gary   Same as them. All of you. Chattin' shit. All day long.
Mouths moving but it's just: chat, chat, chat. Shit, shit, shit.

Tom   No, no.

Gary   Yeah, yeah.

Tom   No.

Gary   Yeah.

Ray   Fight fight fight.

Stephen   Fight fight fight.

Ray   Fight fight fight.

Stephen   Fight.

Tom *pushes* **Gary**.

Ray   Thass it.

Stephen   Do it back or you're gay.

Gary   Fuck's sake.

Gary *pushes* **Tom**.

Ray   Fucking insulted you, man. The gay boy insulted you.

Stephen   Batty hit yer.

Ray   Get him.

Tom   Listen –

Ray   Use your fist.

Stephen   Fist for the battyboy.

Gary   Go on.

Tom   Yeah?

Gary   Do what they tell you. Do what they want to.

Tom   Yeah?

Gary   Follow the leader.

Tom   Yeah.

Tom *punches* **Gary** *in the stomach*.

Ray   Respec', man.

Stephen   Total respec'.

Gary   Fuck you.

Gary *punches* **Tom** *in the stomach very hard.* **Tom** *falls over.*

Ray   Nasty.

Enter **Amy**, **Kerry**, **Alicia**, **Chantal**. **Chantal** *carries the baby.*

Kerry   You're not carrying her properly.

Chantal   Leave it, Kez.

Kerry   But you're not doing the head right.

Chantal   It's my baby, Kez.

Kerry   I know.

Chantal   Yesterday it was yours and now it's mine.

Kerry   I'm only telling you.

Chantal   An' I can do whatever I want with it.

Amy   She's got withdrawal symptoms.

Chantal   Over plastic?

Kerry   Don't say that. You're not fit.

Alicia   Iss the Blazin' Squad. You mellowin'?

Ray   Totally chilled, me darlin'.

Stephen   Totally.

Alicia   Sweet.

Ray   Hear Tom was round yours last night.

Amy   Thass right.

Ray   Gettin' jiggy.

Amy   Do what?

Ray   Jiggy-jiggy-jiggy.

Stephen   Jiggy-jiggy-jiggy.

Amy   You say that?

Tom No.

Ray What? You never?

Amy Thass right.

Ray What? He not fit enough for you?

Amy Iss not that.

Ray You frigid? She frigid, Tom?

Tom No.

Ray Wass wrong with 'em? Why ain't they gettin' jiggy?

Alicia I dunno.

Ray Thass gay.

Tom What?

Ray Youse two are so gay.

Tom/Amy No.

Ray Oooo – sore.

Amy Your ear's started.

Tom Yeah?

Amy You started bleeding again.

Alicia Shit. There's blood.

Kerry I don't wanna look.

Amy You wanna look after that. You got a hanky?

Tom No.

Amy Chantal?

Chantal Here.

Chantal *tucks the baby under her arm to find a paper hanky.*

Kerry You can't do that.

Chantal Juss for a moment.

Kerry   You got to hold it properly all day long.

Chantal   Juss while I'm lookin'.

Kerry   Give it me. Give it me.

Kerry *takes the baby from* **Chantal**. **Chantal** *finds the hanky, passes it to* **Amy**. **Amy** *holds the hanky on* **Tom***'s ear.*

Kerry (*to baby*)   Alright. Alright.

Amy   You wanna hold that there?

Ray   She bite you?

Stephen   Yeah.

Ray   While you were doing it?

Tom   It'll be alright now.

Amy   You sure?

Tom   Yeah.

Tom *continues to hold the handkerchief on his ear.*

Chantal   Give me the baby, Kerry.

Kerry   Later.

Chantal   Now.

Kerry   Bit longer.

Chantal   I gotta have it for Life Skills.

Kerry   I know.

Chantal   So . . . ?

Alicia   Give it, Kez.

Kerry   Juss . . . do the head properly.

Chantal   Alright.

Kerry *hands* **Chantal** *the baby*.

Alicia   Thass it. Come on.

Exit **Alicia**, **Kerry**, **Chantal**.

Amy   Laters.

Exit **Amy**.

Ray   How do you do the ear? She do that ear? Was she like eatin' you?

Tom   Won't stop bleeding.

Ray   What do you do?

Tom   It was . . . we were doing an earring?

Ray   Earring? Earring? Earring? Shit man. In that ear? You was doing an earring in that ear? Shit, man. Thass the gay side. Shit. You was doing an earring in the gay side. Shit.

Stephen   Shit.

Tom   No. No. I'm jokin'. It was –

Ray   Yeah? Yeah?

Tom   It wasn't –

Ray   Yeah? Yeah?

Tom   It was bitin'.

Ray   Yeah?

Stephen   Yeah?

Tom   It was like love-biting.

Ray   I knew it.

Stephen   Thass right.

Tom   We were gettin' hot and biting and that and we –

Ray   Yeah?

Tom   And we got –

Stephen   Jiggy.

Tom   Yeah. Jiggy.

Ray   I knew it.

Tom   Yeah, totally jiggy. Like ridin' and ridin' and ridin'.

Ray   Oh yeah.

Tom   And she was wantin' it.

Stephen   Yeah.

Tom   And I was givin' like, like, like, like –

Ray   Yeah.

Tom   A big man.

Ray   Thass right. Big man.

Stephen   Big man.

Ray   Big man.

Stephen   Big man.

Ray   Big man.

Stephen   Big man.

Gary   Hey – that's sweet.

Ray   Shut it, gay boy.

Stephen   The big man is talkin', battyboy.

Ray   Out of ten?

Tom   She's a six.

Ray   So you see her again?

Tom   Maybe. I'm thinkin' about it.

Stephen   De Clerk.

Ray   Run.

Gary   Give us a hand.

Ray   On your own, man.

Ray *and* **Stephen** *exit rapidly.* **Tom** *goes to help* **Gary**. *Enter* **De Clerk**.

De Clerk   Tom.

Tom   Sir?

De Clerk   A word – now. Gary – move.

Gary   Sir.

De Clerk   You're a stoner, Gary.

Gary   The herb is the people's weed.

De Clerk   Piss off.

Exit **Gary**. **De Clerk** *pulls out a piece of coursework.*

De Clerk   What's this, Tom?

Tom   My Citizenship, sir.

De Clerk   Your Citizenship coursework. And what's this?

Tom   Blood, sir.

De Clerk   Blood on your Citizenship coursework. Blood on the work which tomorrow inspectors are going to want to see.

Tom   I know, sir.

De Clerk   And it's not going to be you that's going to be bollocked, is it? No. It's going to be me. Didn't I say, didn't I say many, many – oh so many – times that your coursework should be neat?

Tom   Yes, sir.

De Clerk   Because I don't need the hassle from the inspectors. Because I'm very stressed out. I'm not sleeping. I told you all that I wasn't sleeping. Some nights nothing. Some nights just a couple of hours.

Tom   I know, sir.

De Clerk   The Head gives me grief, kids give me grief. And now tomorrow the inspection team arrives and what do I find?

Tom   I'm sorry, sir.

De Clerk   I find that you have been bleeding all over 'What Does a Multicultural Society Mean to Me?'.

Tom   I didn't mean to.

De Clerk   I'm not showing this to the inspectors. You can stay behind tonight and copy this out.

Tom   But sir –

De Clerk   You want me to copy it out? I've got lesson plans, marking. I'm going to be here till midnight. I'm not copying it out. You'll see me at the end of school and you'll copy this out.

Tom   Yes, sir.

De Clerk   Right then. See you tonight.

Exit **De Clerk**. **Tom** *mops his ear. The bleeding has stopped. Enter* **Amy**.

Amy   Why you tell 'em you slept with me?

Tom   I never.

Amy   Don't lie. You tole Ray and Steve. Now they tole everyone.

Tom   I'm sorry.

Amy   But it's not true.

Tom   I know.

Amy   So why you – ? You gotta sort out what you are, Tom. You straight? You gay?

Tom   Don't say it in school.

Amy   You bisexual? If you want you can see my therapist. My mum'll sort it out.

Tom   I don't need a therapist.

Amy   I know somewhere they do tarot. The card might tell you.

Tom   I don't believe in that.

Amy   What you gonna do, Tom? You gotta stop lying. You gotta decide what you are.

Tom   I know.

Three

Tom *and* **De Clerk**. **Tom** *holds a bloody handkerchief to his ear.*

Tom   I'm still bleeding, sir.

De Clerk   Just – copy it out.

Tom   I am. I'm just . . . worried.

De Clerk   Mmmmmm.

Tom   You know – worried that I might copy it but then I might drip blood on the, like, copy, you know.

De Clerk   Well, don't.

Tom   I'm trying, only –

De Clerk   Put the paper over there, lean your head over there.

Tom   Alright. (*Does this.*) It feels really weird, sir.

De Clerk   Shut up.

Tom   I'm not writing straight, sir.

De Clerk   Do the best you can.

Tom   I'm trying hard but it's not going straight, sir.

De Clerk   Fuck's sake, Tom.

Tom   Thought so. I just dripped. Blood on the folder.

De Clerk   Haven't you got a plaster?

Tom   I asked at the front office, but the rules say we have to provide our own.

De Clerk   Well, alright – just try not to drip any more.

Tom   Doing my best.

De Clerk's *mobile rings.*

Tom   You gonna get that, sir?

De Clerk   No.

Mobile stops.

Tom   Might have been important.

De Clerk   Nothing else matters. Nothing else matters but your coursework and the inspectors and that we don't become a failing school, okay? There is nothing else in the whole wide world that matters apart from that.

Mobile rings again.

Tom   They don't think so.

Clerk   Well fuck 'em, fuck 'em, fuck 'em.

Tom   They really want to talk to you.

De Clerk   Uhhh.

He answers the mobile.

No. Still at – I told you. I told you. Because we've got the inspectors. No. No. Well, put it in the fridge and I'll . . . put it in the bin. I don't care. I don't care. I can't.

He ends the call.

Tom   Are you married, sir?

De Clerk   I'm not talking any more.

Tom   I was just wondering.

De Clerk   Well, don't.

Tom   Other teachers say: my wife this or my girlfriend that. But you never do.

De Clerk   Well, that's up to them.

Tom   It makes you wonder. We all wonder.

De Clerk   Listen, I'm here from eight in the morning until eight in the evening, midnight the last few weeks – maybe I don't have a personal life.

Tom   Yeah.

De Clerk   Maybe I'm not a person at all. Maybe I'm just lesson plans and marking.

Tom   Yeah. Maybe.

De Clerk   Oh. My head. Have you got a Nurofen?

Tom   Sorry, sir?

De Clerk   Have you got a Nurofen or something?

Tom   No, sir. I had some but I took them all.

De Clerk   Right.

Tom   If you want to go home – go home to your . . . pa.

De Clerk   I can't.

Tom   I can do a massage, sir. I know how to do a massage.

De Clerk   No.

Tom   It stops headaches. I done it loads of times.

De Clerk   Listen. Physical contact is –

Tom   Out of lessons now.

De Clerk   Difficult.

Tom   Shhhhhh. Our secret.

He moves over to **De Clerk** *and massages his shoulders and neck.*

Tom   You've got to breathe too. Remember to keep breathing.

De Clerk   Mmmmm.

Tom   There's a lot of stress about, isn't there?

De Clerk   It's all stress.

Tom   How old are you?

De Clerk   Twenty-two.

Tom   Lots of teachers burn out before they're twenty-five because of all the stress.

De Clerk   Mmmmm.

Tom   You're quite developed, sir. Do you go to the gym?

De Clerk   Sometimes.

Tom   With your . . . partner.

De Clerk   Back to your work now. That was wrong. Physical contact.

Tom   Sir – I'm really sorry, but I've –

Tom *wipes* **De Clerk***'s shoulder.*

Tom   I've dripped on you, sir.

De Clerk   What?

Tom   You've got blood on your shirt.

De Clerk   Oh fuck.

Tom   I'm really sorry. It's a really nice shirt.

De Clerk   Shit. Shit. Shit.

He scrubs at his shoulder.

Tom   If you want me to get you another one, sir –

De Clerk   No no.

Tom   I get a discount. My brother manages Top Man.

De Clerk   Tom – get on with your work. You get on with your work and I'll get on with my work.

Tom   You've got good clothes, sir. For a teacher.

De Clerk   Tom.

Pause.

Tom   Sir . . . I keep on having this dream and in this dream I'm being kissed.

De Clerk   Don't.

Tom   Only I never know whether it's a man or woman who's doing the kissing.

De Clerk   This isn't Biology. I'm Citizenship.

Tom   I think I dream about being kissed by a man.

De Clerk   I don't want to know about that.

Tom   I really want to know: so I dream about a man kissing me?

De Clerk   Please. Don't do this. I'm tired. I'm exhausted. I've got the Head of Department chasing me. I've got the inspectors coming after me like wolves after blood. I've still got eight hours of paperwork. And I've done a full day's teaching. Please understand the pressure I'm under and just copy the work.

Tom   What do you do if you're gay, sir?

De Clerk   You talk to someone.

Tom   I'm trying to talk to you.

De Clerk   You don't talk to me. Talk to your form tutor.

Tom   He hates me.

De Clerk   I don't think so.

Tom   What do you do at the weekends, sir?

De Clerk   Alright. Go away. Go home.

Tom   What about the coursework?

De Clerk   I'll explain the blood to the inspectors.

Tom   Alright then.

He packs up his bag

Bye then, sir.

De Clerk   Bye, Tom.

Tom   I want to talk to someone gay, sir. I don't know any.

De Clerk   Shut up, please shut up.

Tom   I really want to meet someone gay and ask them what it's like.

De Clerk   Well – it's fine. It's normal. It's just fine.

Tom   You reckon?

De Clerk   You know the school policy: we celebrate difference. You report bullies. Everything's okay. You're okay.

Tom   I don't feel okay.

De Clerk   Well – you should do.

Four

Gary, **Tom**. *Smoking a joint.*

Gary   Was it good?

Tom   What?

Gary   You know – when you done Amy?

Tom   Well . . .

Gary   Cos lovin'. There's so many types of lovin'.

Tom   Yeah?

Gary   Yeah. Between man and woman. There's so many types of lovin', in't there?

Tom   You reckon?

Gary   Oh yeah. There's sweet lovin' and there's animal lovin' and there's hard lovin' and there's dirty lovin'. There's millions of ways of lovin'. You follow?

Tom   I think so.

Gary   You lie.

Tom   No.

Gary   I'm chattin' shit, aren't I?

Tom   No.

Gary   Yeah, I'm chattin' shit. Thass the herb. I always chat shit when I'm blazin'. But thass the way I like it. I like to chat shit.

Tom   I like the way you talk.

Gary   Yeah?

Tom   You talk good. You're better than the knobheads. Ray, Steve – they're knobheads.

Gary   Then how come you –

Tom   Yeah yeah.

Gary   – hit me when they tell you?

Tom   I'm sorry.

Gary   No worries. Love and understanding. Peace to you, brother.

Tom   Yeah, peace.

Gary   To mellow, man. Love you, brother.

Tom   Yeah. Brother love.

Gary *puts his arm round* **Tom**.

Gary   You like the brother love?

Tom   Yeah, it's good.

Gary   Peace on the planet. No war. Herb bring harmony. Blaze some more?

Tom   Yeah.

Gary *produces another rolled joint from a tin.*

Gary   So tell me 'bout your lovin'?

Tom   Well –

Gary   Is she your woman now?

Tom   Well –

Gary   Or was it like a one-night lovin' ting?

Tom   Well –

Gary   Don't be shy. Take a big draw and tell.

He hands **Tom** *the joint.* **Tom** *draws.*

Gary   Harder, man. Draw as deep as you can.

Tom *draws as hard as he can.*

Tom   I need some water.

Gary   No. Not till you tell. Tell me what it was like. Come on, man.

Tom   I feel ill.

Gary   I gotta know. I gotta know about the ride.

Gary *pins* **Tom** *to the floor, knees over his arms, sitting on his chest.*

Gary   What was it like when you rode the woman?

Tom   Get off me – off me.

Gary   Jiggy-jiggy with the honey. Ya!

Tom   Off.

He pushes **Gary** *off.*

Tom   I never, alright? I never –

Gary   What?

Tom   I never done her. We never done anything.

Gary   What? Nothing? Oral? Finger?

Tom   Nothing, okay. We never done it.

Gary   Shit. You lied.

Tom   Yeah.

Gary   That's sad, man.

Tom   Yeah, it's really sad.

Gary   So – you not gonna tell me 'bout no lovin'?

Tom   No.

Gary   Shit, broth'. That was gonna be my wank tonight.

Tom   Yeah?

Gary   Yeah – your booty grindin' her. That was gonna –

Tom   Well, there's nothing.

Gary   You wanna pretend for me? Like make it up. So – you never done it. But you can make up like a story, like a dirty story so I got summat in my head.

Tom   I'm not good at stories.

Gary   Just make it dirty so I got something for tonight.

Tom   I'm still supposed to copy out my Citizenship for De Clerk.

Gary   Okay – tell me about your dreams. You gotta have dirty dreams.

Tom   Course.

Gary   Then tell me –

Tom   I don't know.

Gary   Come, brother love. (*Sits* **Tom** *down, puts his arms around him.*) Tell your brother.

Tom   . . . I have this dream. And in this dream I'm lying in bed. Not in my room. Not like my room at home. Like a strange room.

Gary   Like a dungeon?

Tom   No, maybe like a Travel Lodge or something, I don't know.

Gary   Right.

Tom   And I'm almost asleep but then the door opens and this stranger comes into the room.

Gary   Like a thief?

Tom   Maybe but this . . . person, they come over to the bed and they kiss me.

Gary   Right. And – ?

Tom   It's a person but I don't know, I don't know –

Gary   Yeah.

Tom   See, this person, are they a woman or are they . . . ?

Gary   Yeah?

Tom *leans over and kisses* **Gary** *on the lips.*

Gary   You're battyman?

Tom   I don't know.

Gary   Shit, blud, you're battyman. The battyman kissed me. Shit.

Gary *moves away and takes several draws.*

Tom   I don't know. Don't know. Just wanted to see, you know – just wanted to see what it felt like if I –

Gary   And did you like it?

Tom   I don't know.

Gary   Was my lips sweet?

Tom   I don't know.

Gary   No, blud, thass cool, thass cool, I can handle that. Peace to all. Everybody's different. I can go with that.

Tom   I'm sorry.

Gary   Hey – love you still, bro'.

He hugs **Tom***.*

Tom   I just thought – you're Gay Gary.

Gary   Thass just a name. You touch my arse I kill you, see?

Tom   Okay.

Gary   No, see, I like the honeys. You should see my site. Thass where I live out what's in my head, see?

He gets out his laptop, opens his website.

See, these are my fantasies. And I share him with the world on my message board. I got graphics, see?

Tom   Is that you?

Gary   Yeah.

Tom   You got muscles.

Gary   Yeah, well – thass me older, see. And thass my dick.

Tom (*laughs*)   I thought it was a weapon.

Gary (*laughs*)   Yeah. My dick's a lethal weapon. And I fight my way through the desert, see, through all the terrorists and that, see? Nuke nuke nuke. And then when I get to the city – there's all the honeys, see? And I ride 'em, see. And then I kill 'em.

Tom   That's sick, man. I thought you was all love and understanding.

Gary   Can't help what's in my head. Gotta let it out.

Tom   All that – it's . . . wrong.

Gary   Stuff that's in my head. I don't fight it. I let it out. Thass your problem. What's in your head, Tom? Who do you want? The honey or the homo?

Tom   I dunno yet. I want to find out. I gotta try different stuff.

Gary   You wanna get online.

Tom   You reckon?

Gary   Yeah. You start searchin', chatting, message boards, stuff. You can try everything.

Tom   Yeah?

Gary   You wanna do a search now? 'Gay sex'? 'Battyman'?

Tom   No.

Gary   What you want?

Tom   I don't know. Maybe I'll do Amy.

Gary   You reckon?

Tom   I could do if I wanted to, yeah.

Five

Tom *and* **Amy**. **Tom** *carries hair dye.* **Amy** *has a bandage round her wrist.*

Tom   See? It's baby blonde.

Amy   Right.

Tom   I wanna go baby blonde.

Amy   Right.

Tom   And I want you to do it to me.

Amy   I'm supposed to be doing my affirmations.

Tom   What's that?

Amy   I'm supposed to write out a hundred times 'I'm surrounded by love'.

Tom   Why?

Amy   Cos I cut myself again last night.

Tom   Why?

Amy   I dunno. I was bored. Or something. Or stress. I dunno.

Tom   You gotta know.

Amy   I don't. Mum took me down the healer and she told me I had to do the affirmations.

Tom   You can do them later. Do my hair.

Amy   They don't work anyway.

Tom   No?

Amy   I did them before and they never worked.

Tom   What works?

Amy   I dunno. Melissa says I need a shag.

Tom   Maybe you do.

Amy   You reckon?

Tom   Yeah. I reckon.

Amy   There's no one fancies me.

Tom   That's not true.

Amy   Says who?

Tom   Says me.

Amy   Yeah?

Tom   You gonna do my hair?

Amy   If you want.

Tom   We need a bowl of water.

Amy   Alright.

Tom   And a towel.

Amy   Yeah yeah.

Tom   Thanks.

Amy *exits.* **Tom** *removes his shirt. Folds it up. Arranges himself on the floor. Pause. Enter* **Melissa**.

Melissa   Alright?

Tom   Alright.

Melissa   You seen my iPod?

Tom   No.

Melissa   She takes my iPod. Drives me mental. We're always having words. There'll be a ruck soon.

Tom   Right.

Melissa   You shagging?

Tom   Not yet.

Melissa   Do us all a favour and give her one, will you?

Tom   Do my best.

Melissa   Where the fuck's it gone?

Exit **Melissa**. **Tom** *arranges himself again on the floor to look as alluring and yet as natural as possible for* **Amy**. *Enter* **Amy** *with bowl of water and towel.*

Amy   I got it.

Tom   I took my top off.

Amy   Right.

Tom   Cos I don't want to get bleach on it.

Amy   Right.

Tom   That alright? Me getting naked?

Amy   Whatever. You got the instructions?

Tom   Yeah.

He gives **Amy** *the instructions.*

Tom   I've been thinking about what you said.

Amy (*reading instructions*)   Yeah?

Tom   About sorting myself out and that. In my head. You know – about whether I wanted . . . you.

Amy   You seen a therapist?

Tom   No. I just been thinking.

Amy   Right.

Tom   About who I wanna kiss and that.

Amy   Right. You got any allergies?

Tom   Why?

Amy   Cos it says here – (*the instructions*) You got any allergies?

Tom   Dust and peanuts.

Amy   Dust and peanuts should be alright. You wanna get started?

Tom   If you like. What if you got bleach on your top?

Amy   It's a crap top.

Tom   Yeah, but you'd ruin it. Bleach down the front.

Amy   Mum'll recycle it.

Tom   Maybe you better take your top off too.

Amy   I don't think so.

Tom   Go on. I took my top off. Time you took your top off too.

Amy   No.

Tom   Come on. Take it off. Take it off.

Tom *reaches out to* **Amy** *– she pushes him away.*

Amy   I'm not taking my top off, alright?

Tom   Alright. Do you reckon I should go down the gym?

Amy   I don't know.

Tom   Maybe I should go down the gym. My body's stupid.

Amy   No.

Tom   I've got a stupid body.

Amy   No. You've got a fit body. I like your body.

Tom   Yeah?

Amy   It's a nice body.

Tom   Do you wanna touch it?

Amy   I dunno.

Tom   Come on. Touch it if you like.

Amy   Alright.

Amy *reaches out to touch* **Tom**. *Enter* **Melissa** *followed by* **Chantal**, **Kerry** *and* **Alicia**. **Alicia** *carries the baby.*

Melissa   Your mates are here. They're shagging.

Exit **Melissa**.

Chantal/Kerry/Alicia   Alright?

Tom   Alright.

Amy   We're not – we weren't gonna –

Chantal   Thass a buff bod.

Tom   Yeah?

Chantal   For a kid, you're fit. He's fit, isn't he?

Kerry   He's alright. I mean I wouldn't –

Amy   We weren't gonna –

Kerry   But yeah, he's alright.

Amy   I was gonna dye his hair.

Chantal   Go on then.

Tom   Forget it.

Chantal   No. Go on.

Tom   Another time. I don't want people watching.

Chantal   It's safe. Go on. We heard you cut yourself again. You alright?

Amy   Oh yeah. I'm fine. Come on – let's wash your hair.

Amy *pours water over* **Tom**'s *head*.

Tom   Owww! Hurts! Awwww! Burning, aagh!

Amy   Shit.

Tom   What you – ? You put cold in that? You never put any cold in that.

Amy   I forgot.

Tom   You forgot. Shit. I'm gonna be scarred. Ugh.

Amy   I'll get cold.

She runs out with the jug. **Tom** *paces around scratching at his scalp, groaning.* **Alicia** *get out cigarettes.*

Kerry   Lish – don't.

Alicia   What?

Kerry   Not around the kid.

Alicia   Don't be stupid.

Kerry   It stunts 'em.

Alicia   Thass when you're pregnant.

Kerry   Not when you're mother.

She takes the packet of cigarettes from **Alicia**.

Alicia   Fuck's sake. I get stressed out without 'em.

Kerry   Yeah – well.

Alicia   See that, Spazz? Took my fags.

Kerry   Don't call it that.

Alicia   Whatever.

Enter **Amy** *with jug of cold water.*

Amy   Here.

Tom *kneels in front of bowl.* **Amy** *pours cold water over his head.*

Tom   Aggghhhh.

He lies back.

Amy   You better now.

Tom   Is there red? Like burns?

Amy   A bit.

Tom   Thought so.

Chantal   Are you gonna shag? Cos we can leave it you're gonna shag.

Tom   No. We're not gonna shag.

Chantal   You sure?

Tom   Yeah. I'm sure. We're not gonna shag. We're never gonna . . . no.

Six

Tom, Tarot Reader. *Nine cards spread out in a fan – three lines of three.*

Tarot Reader   There's the tower. You see? That's the tower. Now – you are facing a moment of great change. A moment of great decision. Would you like to ask me a question?

Tom   I . . . no.

Tarot Reader   Any moment you need to – you must ask me a question.

Tom   Alright.

Tarot Reader   But the tower makes sense to you?

Tom   Yes.

Tarot Reader   The foundation on which – you see here these are your emotions – the foundations on which your emotions are based is unstable. It may collapse at any time.

Tom   Yes. That's how I feel.

Tarot Reader   Then the cards are speaking to you?

Tom   Yes, yes, they are.

Tarot Reader   Good. Good.

Tom   Nothing feels . . . fixed. Everything feels as though it could fall over. I'm confused.

Tarot Reader   Lots of people –

Tom   I don't know who I am. I want to know –

Tarot Reader   That's how lots of people –

Tom   I need to know. I need to choose.

Tarot Reader   Of course, yes yes, but please . . . listen . . . so many people are . . . Nobody knows . . . All the time we're told choose, decide . . .

Tom   Yes.

Tarot Reader   All the time, we've got these choices.

Tom   I know.

Tarot Reader   And we feel so unprepared, but if we explore the choices, if we tune our hearts and our heads to the cards. Do you see? Do you see?

Tom   I think so.

Tarot Reader   Good. Good. Let's look at the future.

Tom   Yes.

Tarot Reader   Now this is – the cards are very strong here.

Tom   That's good.

Tarot Reader   Two of the major . . . we call these the major arcana, you see? Here – the pictures. The High Priestess – here. Drawing back the veil. Drawing back the veil to let you into her world.

Tom   It's a woman?

Tarot Reader   She's a feminine –

Tom   It's a woman letting me into her – I've got to know – that's a woman –

Tarot Reader   It's more complicated than that. Yes, we used to say: the cards are men and they are women. The King. The Queen. But in this day and age – it's more complex – we prefer the masculine and feminine energies.

Tom   But she's a woman.

Tarot Reader   Or a man with a feminine energy.

Tom   Oh.

Tarot Reader   And here – the lovers. You are about to enter the gate, pass the threshold and embrace the lovers. A lover for you. Yes? You've got a question?

Tom   I've really got to know. Is it? Is it a . . . a man or a woman?

Tarot Reader   It's not so simple. Look at the cards. Really listen to the cards. You are about to pass through the gateway and meet your lover. Man or a woman? What do the cards say?

Tom   I can't . . . Nothing.

Tarot Reader   Make yourself comfortable. Be patient. Listen.

Tom   No. I really can't . . .

Tarot Reader   We have time. You will choose a course of action. With the cards you will choose a course of action. Just watch and wait and listen. And listen. Listen. Listen to the cards.

Tom *looks at the cards. Long pause.*

Tarot Reader   Yes?

Tom   Yes.

Tarot Reader   You know what to do?

Tom   I know what to do.

Seven

Tom, **Amy**. **Amy** *carries the baby.*

Tom   You got the baby.

Amy   She made me. Said I'd have detention for a week.

Tom   That's harsh.

Amy   Totally harsh. I told her – I'm not fit to be a mother, look at my arms. You can't be a mother when you've got cuts all over your arms.

Tom   And what did she say?

Amy   Said it would take me out of myself – think about another life.

Tom   Bit of plastic.

Amy   And now I have to write down all my thoughts and feelings in my baby diary.

Tom   What you written?

Amy   Nothing. Don't feel anything. It doesn't do anything. Just sits there. It's heavy.

Tom   Let me feel.

Amy   Go on then.

Amy *gives* **Tom** *the baby.*

Tom   Yeah. Really heavy.

He drops the baby.

Whoops.

Amy   You did that on purpose.

Tom   Maybe.

Amy   You're trouble.

Tom   That's right. Do you reckon it's damaged?

Amy   Shut up.

Tom *picks up the baby.*

Tom   No – it's fine.

Amy   Don't tell Kerry – she'll go mental.

Tom (*to baby*)   You're alright, aren't you? Aren't you? Yes.

Tom *throws the baby up in the air – lets it fall on the floor.*

Amy   You're mad.

Tom   I'm rubbish at catching. Catch it!

Tom *throws the baby to* **Amy**. *She catches it.*

Amy   I'll be bollocked if it's damaged.

Tom   Throw it to me. Come on.

Amy *throws the baby. He lets it fall to the floor again.*

Tom   Why can't I catch it?

Amy   You're not trying. Give it here.

She goes to pick up the baby. **Tom** *stops her.*

Tom   No – leave it.

Amy   Why?

Tom   Cos I'm here. You can hold the baby later.

Amy   What am I gonna write in my baby diary?

Tom   Make it up.

He takes his shirt off.

Amy   What are you doing?

Tom   I went down the gym. See?

Amy   How many times you been?

Tom   Three.

Amy   I don't think three's gonna make a difference.

Tom   Course it is. Have a feel.

Amy   Yeah?

Tom *flexes a bicep.*

Tom   Feel that.

Amy   Alright.

Amy *feels his bicep.*

Tom   See?

Amy   What?

Tom   It's stronger. Harder.

Amy   You reckon?

Tom   Oh yeah – that's much harder.

Amy   I dunno.

She picks up the baby.

Tom   Do you wanna have sex?

Amy   Maybe.

Tom   I think maybe we should have sex.

Amy   I've never had sex before.

Tom   Neither have I. I've seen it online.

Amy   Yeah?

Tom   Round Gary's.

Amy   Gay Gary's?

Tom   He's not gay.

Amy   Right. Are you gay?

Tom   Come here.

Amy *goes to* **Tom***. He takes the baby out of her arms and lays it on the floor. They kiss.*

Tom   Did you like that?

Amy   Yeah. Is it me?

Tom   What?

Amy   In your dreams? Is it me you're kissing in your dream?

Tom   No.

Amy   Are you sure? If you can't see the face . . . ?

Tom   Yeah, well. But I can feel it.

Amy   And it's not me?

Tom   It's not you. Does that bother you?

Amy   No.

Tom   Good.

They kiss again.

Melissa (*off*)   Amy.

Amy   What?

Melissa (*off*)   You got my camcorder?

Amy   No.

Melissa (*off*)   You sure? I can't find it anywhere.

Amy   I'm sure.

Melissa (*off*)   If you've taken it again . . .

Amy   I haven't taken it again.

Melissa (*off*)   I'm coming to look.

Amy   No.

Exit **Amy**. **Tom** *waits. Enter* **De Clerk**.

Tom   How did you get in here, sir?

De Clerk   Through the floor.

Tom   What? You just . . . ?

De Clerk   Come through the floor.

Tom   Shit.

De Clerk   Just something I can do. Don't tell the Head. We're not supposed to have special powers.

Tom   Alright. Are you here cos I'm still a bit gay – is that it?

De Clerk   Let's not talk about that.

Tom   I sort of decided I wasn't gonna be gay any more – now you sort of – well, it's a bit gay, isn't it, coming through the floor like that?

De Clerk   Are you going to have sex with her?

Tom   Yeah, I reckon. What – don't you think I should?

De Clerk   We can't tell you yes or no. That's not what we do.

Tom   Why not?

De Clerk   Because you have to make your own choices.

Tom   But why? Everything's so confusing. There's so many choices. I don't feel like a person. I just feel like all these bits floating around. And none of them match up. Like a jigsaw that's never going to be finished. It's doing my head in.

De Clerk   And what would you prefer?

Tom   Someone to tell me what to be.

De Clerk   No one's going to do that.

Tom   I wish they would.

De Clerk   When I was growing up: everyone told you who to be. They told you what to do. What was right and what was wrong. What your future would be.

Tom   I'd like that.

De Clerk   No. It made me very unhappy.

Tom   I'm unhappy – too many choices. You were unhappy – no choices. Everyone's unhappy. Life's shit, isn't it, sir?

De Clerk   That is I would say a distinct possibility.

Tom   Are you still unhappy, sir?

De Clerk   If I stop. If I stop working and rushing – the inspection, the continual assessment – trying to pay the mortgage every month, trying to please the Head, trying to get home before nine every night – then, yes, I'm unhappy. But only when I stop.

Tom   You've got a boyfriend?

De Clerk   I can't talk about that.

Tom   You're gay, sir. I don't mean that in a bad way. I just mean – like you know who you are. And you're gay. I'm going to have sex with her.

De Clerk   If that's what you want.

Tom   So you better get back through the floor. I'm not having you watching us.

De Clerk   I don't want to watch. Use protection.

Tom   I know.

De Clerk   If you're having sex, use protection.

Tom   That's telling me what to do.

De Clerk   It's advice.

Tom   It's telling me what to do. You should tell me more of that.

De Clerk   I can't. Promise me you'll use protection.

Tom   I might do.

De Clerk   Promise.

Tom   Do all gay people come through floors?

De Clerk   Now you're being silly.

Enter **Amy**.

Amy   She's gone now.

Tom   Good. (*To* **De Clerk**.) You going?

De Clerk   Take care.

Exit **De Clerk**.

Tom   Is everyone out?

Amy   Yeah. They're all out. Got the place to ourselves.

Tom   That's good.

Amy   Are you scared?

Tom   A bit. Are you?

Amy   Scared and excited.

Tom   We'll take it slow.

Amy   Yeah. Let's take it really slow. You got anything?

Tom   Like what?

Amy   Like condoms and that?

Tom   No.

Amy   Oh.

Tom   Does that bother you?

Amy   No. Does that bother you?

Tom   No.

Amy   Do you love me?

Tom   I don't know. Maybe later. Is that alright?

Amy   Yeah. That's alright.

Tom   After – we can do my hair. I still want blonde hair.

Amy   Alright.

Tom   Turn the light out.

Amy   I want to see you.

Tom   No.

Tom *turns the light off. The* **Baby** *comes forward and speaks to the audience.*

Baby   And so it happened. My mummy and my daddy made me that night. Neither of them enjoyed it very much. But they did it. And that's what they wanted. And that night I started to grow in my mummy's tummy. And by the time she did her GCSEs I was almost ready to come out of her tummy.

I think that night as they lay together in the dark she thought they might spend all their time together from that day on. But that didn't happen. In fact, once that night was over, they were sort of shy and embarrassed whenever they saw each other until – by the time I was born – they weren't speaking to each other at all. And Mummy says for a few moments – she's sure there were a few moments that night when he did really, really love her. And I believe her.

They did talk to each other once more after they left school – but there's one more bit of the story to show you before we get to that.

Eight

Tom *and* **Martin**. **Tom** *has a hat pulled down, completely covering his hair.*

Tom   You've got a nice place.

Martin (*off*)   Thank you.

Tom   Yeah, really nice. Trendy.

Martin (*off*)   Thank you.

Tom   What do you do?

Martin (*off*)   My job?

Tom   Yeah. Your job.

Martin (*off*)   I'm a systems analyst.

Tom   Right. Right. Is that alright?

Martin (*off*)   I enjoy it.

Tom   And the pay's good?

Martin (*off*)   The pay is ridiculously good.

Tom   Well – that's good.

Martin (*off*)   And you?

Tom   What?

Martin (*off*)   Do you have a job?

Tom   Yes.

Martin (*off*)   What do you do?

Tom   Well, actually, I'm looking.

Martin (*off*)   I see.

Enter **Martin**, *with two bottles of beer. He gives one of the bottles of beer to* **Tom**.

Martin   Cheers.

Tom   Right. Cheers.

Martin   If you want to take off –

Tom   I'm alright.

Martin   Maybe – your hat . . . ?

Tom   No.

Martin   Alright.

Tom   It's just I had a disaster.

Martin   Yes?

Tom   With my hair.

Martin   I see.

Tom   Yeah, this mate tried to dye my hair but it went wrong.

Martin   Right.

Tom   Yeah, tried to dye my hair, but I had a bit of a reaction and it's gone really weird, like ginger bits and green bits and that. Last month. I'm waiting for it to grow out. I look weird so that's why I'm wearing –

Martin   It suits you.

Tom   Yeah?

Martin   The hat. It's a good look.

Tom   Thank you.

Martin   You're a good-looking guy.

Tom   Right.

Martin   Was it your boyfriend?

Tom   What?

Martin   With the hair dye?

Tom   No.

Martin   Have you got a boyfriend?

Tom   No. Have you?

Martin   Yes. Is that alright?

Tom   I suppose. How old are you?

Martin   Twenty-one.

Tom   Right.

Martin   How old are you?

Tom   Eighteen.

Martin   You said nineteen in the chatroom.

Tom   Did I?

Martin   Yes.

Tom   Well, I'm eighteen.

Martin   But actually you look younger.

Tom   Really?

Martin   You actually look about sixteen.

Tom   Everyone says I look younger. That's what they said when I was at school.

Martin   Right. Do you want to come through to the bedroom?

Tom   In a minute. Are you happy?

Martin   What?

Tom   You know, in your life and that? Does it make you happy?

Martin   I suppose so.

Tom   With your boyfriend and your job and that?

Martin   I never really think about it.

Tom   You seem happy.

Martin   Then I suppose I am.

Tom   That's good.

Martin   And you?

Tom   What?

Martin   Are you happy?

Tom   I reckon. Yes, I am.

Martin   Well, that's good. Look, we really should get into the bedroom –

Tom   Right.

Martin   My boyfriend's coming back at five and I don't want to –

Tom   Right.

Martin   Sorry to hurry you, but –

Tom   That's alright.

Martin   You can keep your hat on.

Tom   Thanks.

Martin   You're cute.

Tom   Thanks. I've never done this before.

Martin   Chatrooms?

Tom   This. All of it.

Martin   Sex?

Tom   No. I've done sex. Only . . .

Martin   Not with someone so old?

Tom   Not with . . .

Martin   Twenty-two too old for you?

Tom   No. Not with . . . a bloke. I mean, I did it with girls, a girl, but . . .

Martin   Did you like it?

Tom   It was alright.

Martin   If you like that kind of thing.

Tom   Yeah. I'm shaking. Sorry. I feel nervous. Is it gonna hurt?

Martin   Not if we do it right.

Tom   How will we know?

Martin   I don't know. You just have to . . . er . . . suck it and see.

Tom (*laughs*)   You dirty bastard.

Martin   Yeah.

Tom   I shouldn't have come.

Martin   Alright then – another time. How are you getting back?

Tom   No, no.

He kisses **Martin**.

Martin   Mixed messages.

Tom   You're right. I'm sixteen.

Martin   I know.

Tom   I'm legal.

Martin   What do you want?

Tom   This.

He kisses **Martin**.

Tom   Come on then. Where's the bedroom? Or do you want your boyfriend to find out?

Martin   The bedroom's through there.

Tom   Your boyfriend, he's not . . . ?

Martin   Yes?

Tom   He's not . . . is your boyfriend a teacher?

Martin (*laughs*)   God, no. He's a mortgage broker. Why?

Tom   Nothing.

Martin   Ready?

Tom   Ready. Just – don't touch my hat, alright?

Martin   Alright.

Nine

Amy, **Tom**.

Amy   Your hair's alright.

Tom   Yeah. Took a few months. But in the end it went back to normal.

Amy   You should still do an earring.

Tom   You reckon?

Amy   Yeah. I always reckoned an earring would really suit you.

Tom   Maybe one day.

Amy   Yeah. One day. What you up to?

Tom   Not much. I'm going to college next year.

Amy   That's good.

Tom   Fashion.

Amy   Nice.

Tom   And I'm doing coat-check.

Amy   In a club?

Tom   Sort of pub-club.

Amy   Gay club?

Tom   Just Fridays and Saturdays. You should come along. It's a laugh.

Amy   You got a boyfriend?

Tom   I dunno.

Amy   You got to know.

Tom   There's a bloke . . . We . . . meet up. A couple of times a week. But he's living with someone.

Amy   His boyfriend.

Tom   Yeah. He's got a boyfriend. He keeps on saying they're gonna split but they haven't. Still – we have a laugh. He's got money.

Amy   Right.

Tom   You seeing anyone?

Amy   Yeah.

Tom   Who?

Amy   Nosy. I mean, I can't go out much but, you know, if I get a babysitter –

Tom   Right.

Amy   I'm gonna do college in a couple of years.

Tom   That's good.

Amy   Just gotta wait till she's a bit older.

Tom   Of course. If you need me to babysit –

Amy   No.

Tom   I don't mind.

Amy   I've got mates do that for me. Kerry loves it.

Tom   Yeah, but if you ever need me to –

Amy   I don't need you to.

Tom   I want to.

Amy   I don't want you to, alright?

Tom   Alright. I still . . . think about you.

Amy   Right.

Tom   Like . . . fancy you and that.

Amy   You told your boyfriend?

Tom   Sometimes, when he kisses me, I think about you. He kisses me but I close my eyes and it's your face I see.

Amy   You can't have it both ways.

Tom   That's what I want.

Amy   Well – you can't have it.

Enter **Gary**, *pushing a pram.*

Gary   Alright, babe?

Amy   Yeah. Alright.

Gary *kisses* **Amy**.

Amy   She been alright?

Gary   Yeah. Fast asleep the whole time.

Amy   She'll be awake all night now.

Gary   You want me to wake her?

Amy   No. Leave her alone.

Gary   Alright, Tom?

Tom   She told me she was going out with someone.

Gary   You guess who?

Tom   No. You gonna bring the kid up to be a stoner too?

Gary   No. I give up the weed, didn't I? Can't be blazing around the kid, can I? Once you got a kid to look after – that's the time to grow up, I reckon.

Tom   Yeah – suppose that's right.

Amy   Tom's gone gay now.

Gary   Thass cool.

Tom   Can I have a look at her?

Amy   We gotta go in a minute. Mum's booked us up the naturopath.

Tom   I just want to have a quick look.

Amy   Go on then.

Tom   She's beautiful.

Amy   Yeah. She's alright.

Tom   Can I pick her up?

Amy   No.

Tom   I'll be careful.

Amy   I don't want you to.

Tom   Alright.

Amy   Not now she's settled.

Tom   Alright.

Amy   Best to leave her alone.

Tom   Alright.

Amy   I want to keep her out of the sun.

Tom   Of course.

Gary   We've got to get the bus.

Amy   Yeah.

Tom   Will I see you again?

Amy   Maybe.

Tom   I wanna see you again. I'm the dad.

Amy   Gary looks after her – don't you?

Gary   Yeah.

Tom   Yeah – but still.

Enter **Martin**.

Martin   Sorry, I tried to get away only –

Martin *goes to kiss* **Tom**. *He steps away.*

Tom   Don't.

Amy   You his boyfriend?

Martin   I wouldn't . . . sort of . . .

Tom   Yeah. Only sort of.

Amy   Better than nothing though, isn't it?

Martin   That's right.

Amy   See ya.

Exit **Amy** *and* **Gary** *with pram.*

Tom   Did you tell him?

Martin   What?

Tom   You know. About me. You were supposed to tell him about me.

Martin   He's away this weekend. What do you want to do?

Tom   Do you love me?

Martin   You know I don't like to use that word.

Tom   Because?

Martin   Because.

Tom   Tell me.

Martin   What does it mean? It doesn't mean anything. 'Love'? It doesn't mean . . .

Tom   You've got to say it.

Martin   No.

Tom   There's no point to this. There's no point to anything. What's the point?

Martin   Money. Sex. Fun. That's the point.

Tom   No. I want –

Martin   What?

Tom   Say you love me.

Martin   No.

Tom   Say you love me.

Martin   No.

Tom   Say you love me. Please. Please. Please – say you love me.

Martin   Okay. I love you – okay?

Beat.

Tom   . . . No.

Martin   Fuck's sake. Why can't you . . . moneysexfun?

Tom   Because I want more. I want everything. I want . . .

Martin   Yes?

Tom   I want everything and I want . . . I want . . . I want to find out everything.

Martin (*laughs*)   You're a baby. Treat you like a baby.

Tom   No. Not any more. No.

Methuen Drama Modern Plays

include work by

Edward Albee
Jean Anouilh
John Arden
Margaretta D'Arcy
Peter Barnes
Sebastian Barry
Brendan Behan
Dermot Bolger
Edward Bond
Bertolt Brecht
Howard Brenton
Anthony Burgess
Simon Burke
Jim Cartwright
Caryl Churchill
Noël Coward
Lucinda Coxon
Sarah Daniels
Nick Darke
Nick Dear
Shelagh Delaney
David Edgar
David Eldridge
Dario Fo
Michael Frayn
John Godber
Paul Godfrey
David Greig
John Guare
Peter Handke
David Harrower
Jonathan Harvey
Iain Heggie
Declan Hughes
Terry Johnson
Sarah Kane
Charlotte Keatley
Barrie Keeffe
Howard Korder

Robert Lepage
Doug Lucie
Martin McDonagh
John McGrath
Terrence McNally
David Mamet
Patrick Marber
Arthur Miller
Mtwa, Ngema & Simon
Tom Murphy
Phyllis Nagy
Peter Nichols
Sean O'Brien
Joseph O'Connor
Joe Orton
Louise Page
Joe Penhall
Luigi Pirandello
Stephen Poliakoff
Franca Rame
Mark Ravenhill
Philip Ridley
Reginald Rose
Willy Russell
Jean-Paul Sartre
Sam Shepard
Wole Soyinka
Shelagh Stephenson
Peter Straughan
C. P. Taylor
Theatre de Complicite
Theatre Workshop
Sue Townsend
Judy Upton
Timberlake Wertenbaker
Roy Williams
Snoo Wilson
Victoria Wood

Methuen Drama Film titles include

Methuen Drama Contemporary Dramatists

include

John Arden (two volumes)
Arden & D'Arcy
Peter Barnes (three volumes)
Sebastian Barry
Dermot Bolger
Edward Bond (six volumes)
Howard Brenton
    (two volumes)
Richard Cameron
Jim Cartwright
Caryl Churchill (two volumes)
Sarah Daniels (two volumes)
Nick Darke
David Edgar (three volumes)
Ben Elton
Dario Fo (two volumes)
Michael Frayn (three volumes)
David Greig
John Godber (two volumes)
Paul Godfrey
John Guare
Lee Hall (two volumes)
Peter Handke
Jonathan Harvey
    (two volumes)
Declan Hughes
Terry Johnson (two volumes)
Sarah Kane
Barrie Keefe
Bernard-Marie Koltès
David Lan
Bryony Lavery
Deborah Levy
Doug Lucie

David Mamet (four volumes)
Martin McDonagh
Duncan McLean
Anthony Minghella
    (two volumes)
Tom Murphy (four volumes)
Phyllis Nagy
Anthony Neilsen
Philip Osment
Louise Page
Stewart Parker (two volumes)
Joe Penhall
Stephen Poliakoff
    (three volumes)
David Rabe
Mark Ravenhill
Christina Reid
Philip Ridley
Willy Russell
Eric-Emmanuel Schmitt
Ntozake Shange
Sam Shepard (two volumes)
Shelagh Stephenson
Wole Soyinka (two volumes)
David Storey (three volumes)
Sue Townsend
Judy Upton
Michel Vinaver
    (two volumes)
Arnold Wesker (two volumes)
Michael Wilcox
Roy Williams
Snoo Wilson (two volumes)
David Wood (two volumes)
Victoria Wood

Methuen Drama World Classics

include

Jean Anouilh (two volumes)
Brendan Behan
Aphra Behn
Bertolt Brecht (eight volumes)
Büchner
Bulgakov
Calderón
Čapek
Anton Chekhov
Noël Coward (eight volumes)
Feydeau
Eduardo De Filippo
Max Frisch
John Galsworthy
Gogol
Gorky (two volumes)
Harley Granville Barker
    (two volumes)
Victor Hugo
Henrik Ibsen (six volumes)
Jarry

Lorca (three volumes)
Marivaux
Mustapha Matura
David Mercer (two volumes)
Arthur Miller (five volumes)
Molière
Musset
Peter Nichols (two volumes)
Joe Orton
A. W. Pinero
Luigi Pirandello
Terence Rattigan
    (two volumes)
W. Somerset Maugham
    (two volumes)
August Strindberg
    (three volumes)
J. M. Synge
Ramón del Valle-Inclán
Frank Wedekind
Oscar Wilde